letters of a
Civil War Surgeon

Major William Watson

letters of a
Civil War Surgeon

Edited by
Paul Fatout

Purdue University Press
West Lafayette, Indiana

01   00   99   98   97   5   4   3   2   1

∞ The paper used in this book meets the minimum requirements of
American National Standard for Information Sciences—Permanence of
Paper for Printed Library Materials, ANSI Z39.48-1992.

Printed in the United States of America
Design by Anita Noble
Sketch of A. R. Waud, "Citizens helping the wounded," from Civil War
Drawings Collection, Prints and Photographs Division, Library of
Congress. Photograph of William Watson courtesy of Pioneer Historical
Society of Bedford County (Pennsylvania).

Library of Congress Cataloging-in-Publication Data
Watson, William, 1837–1879.
    [Correspondence. Selections]
    Letters of a Civil War surgeon / edited by Paul Fatout.
       p.   cm.
    Originally published: [West Lafayette, Ind., 1961]. With new index.
    Includes bibliographical references and index.
    ISBN 1-55753-092-0 (pbk. : alk paper)
    1. Watson, William, 1837–1879—Correspondence. 2. United States,
Army. Pennsylvania Infantry Regiment, 105th (1861–1865) 3. United
States—History—Civil War, 1861–1865—Personal narratives.
    4. United States—History—Civil War, 1861–1865—Medical care.
    5. Pennsylvania—History—Civil War, 1861–1865. 6. Surgeons—
Pennsylvania—Bedford—Correspondence. 7. Bedford (Pa.)—Biography.
    8. United States. Army—Surgeons—Correspondence. I. Fatout, Paul.
    II. Title
    E527.5 105th.W38 1996
    973.7'448—dc20   96-19912
                                                            CIP

1861–1865

To soldiers of all armies,

north and south,

who lived through that war and

who died in it,

this book is dedicated.

Contents

Preface

These letters of Major William Watson, surgeon in the Army of the Potomac from 1862 to 1865, are the property of his grand-niece, Mrs. Margaret Winfield Woodworth, of West Lafayette, Indiana. I am grateful for her kind permission to publish them. My best thanks also to E. R. "Abe" Taylor, a Civil War enthusiast of the Indiana State Police, who informed me of the existence of these letters.

The only editing is minor and mechanical, applied only for convenience in reading. Dr. Watson, like other correspondents, had his idiosyncrasies. Generally writing in a hurry, he did not bother with paragraphing, question marks, apostrophes, or periods after abbreviations. Commas are almost nonexistent and quotation marks are rare. His chief mark resembles a dash that at times was probably intended as a dash, at other times as a period.

Conventional punctuation has been supplied and the occasional misspelling corrected. Otherwise, except for deletion of sections dealing only with family matters, relatives and friends, the letters are reproduced verbatim. Sporadic capitalization has been preserved, though it is often difficult to determine whether or not capitalization was intended.

Considering that many were written hastily under stress of campaigning, the letters are remarkably legible. They are the record of a noncombatant medical officer in the midst of combat. Chiefly concerned with immediate events, he was yet a man of positive convictions and unclouded Union sympathies who expressed views on the larger implications of the war. Major Watson has left us a human narrative derived from almost three years of firsthand experience in the great conflict.

Much of the preparation of this book for the press occurred while I was in Berkeley, California. In this long-distance editing I would have been stymied without the faithful support of Mrs. Richard Beale. I am grateful also to my wife, Roberta, for sterling aid on proofing and indexing.

1862

ON SEPTEMBER 12, 1862, Dr. William Watson, aged twenty-five, of Bedford, Pennsylvania, was detailed as surgeon with the rank of major to the 105th Regiment of Pennsylvania Volunteers. The son of a physician, a graduate of Lafayette College and the medical college of the University of Pennsylvania, the young surgeon was professionally well qualified, and he was also a strong Union man.

The 105th Regiment, organized at Pittsburgh in September–October 1861, had seen service in the defense of Washington and in General George B. McClellan's Peninsula campaign in early 1862, having been blooded at Fair Oaks, Seven Pines, and the Seven Days' battles before Richmond. Afterward it saw action at Malvern Hill and, during John Pope's campaign in northern Virginia, at Bristoe Station, second Bull Run, Chantilly, and elsewhere. When Major Watson joined the regiment, it was a seasoned outfit guarding Potomac fords from the Monocacy River to Conrad's Ferry. A unit of the Army of the

Potomac, the 105th was in the 3rd Corps, Major General
S. P. Heintzelman; 1st Division, Brigadier General David B.
Birney; 1st Brigade, Brigadier General John C. Robinson.
Colonel Amor A. McKnight had been in command of the
regiment since its organization.

Until his discharge on May 27, 1865, Major Watson
sent home many letters: to his father, Dr. William Hartley
Watson; and to his six younger sisters: Ella, Charlotte,
Eliza, Emma, Margaret, and Marie. In these frequent
missives, often hastily scribbled, he has left us a variety
of impressions of camp life, marches, and battles; of the
soldier's matter-of-fact willingness to accept, though not
without grumbling, the rigors of his lot; of concern with
the job at hand and with immediate needs like food and
shelter; of a veteran's indifference to the flag-waving of
professional patriots.

*A*FTER BEING COMMISSIONED by Governor Andrew J.
Curtin, the new surgeon prepared to search for his regiment. From Harrisburg, on September 16, he wrote his
father:

> *I have been detailed to the 105th, Col. McKnight. He is some-*
> *where about Washington or in Maryland about Hagerstown. I*
> *received imperative orders to leave today at one o'clock. But will*
> *not get off until tonight. I go straight to Washington and look*
> *up my Regiment. No one here knows its exact locality. I have*
> *not succeeded yet in getting any Uniform. . . . Tell the Girls I*
> *have not time to get my Photograph taken. But when I am*
> *equipped and have time I will send it them. . . . You had better*

look me up a horse. As Surgeon doubtless I will need one. I will write you particularly about it as soon as I am fixed. Let the Girls write me often.[1]

The "Girls" were his bevy of sisters, from whom he wanted, as soldiers always want, a flow of letters. He went on to the vicinity of Washington, where, trying to locate the 105th Pennsylvania, he coped with the red tape and confusion common to armies and particularly prevalent in the turmoil around the capitol in 1862. He sensed, also, a slight hint of the politicking that, from first to last, beset the Army of the Potomac. On September 17, he wrote:

I arrived in Washington 10 A.M. to day. Did not succeed in getting equipped in Harrisburg—nor am I better off here at present. Immediately on arriving I set about finding my Regt. I went to Alexandria by boat. Then I gave a Livery man five dollars to drive me in search of the Regt. Did not take my baggage with me as I intended returning to Washington to get my outfit. After many hours search I succeeded in overhauling the Regiment and a more dilapidated one I never expect to see. They have been engaged in all the sanguinary Peninsular fights. The tents are nothing but rags affording no protection whatever. The Regt. only numbers three hundred and fifty—all the rest being sick or wounded in the General Hospitals. There are two Assistant Surgeons. The first assistant has been in service since last October. He questioned me closely, asking what Regt. I belonged to previous to promotion. I know by the way he talked that he had expected the position himself. . . . The Regiment is located about seven miles south of Alexandria guarding one of the advanced

forts. . . . The Regiment is attached to General Robinson's Bri-
gade, Kearny's division. I am afraid I will have hard quarters
for awhile if we don't succeed in getting new tents. There is not
a Sibley tent in the whole Regt. After obtaining all the informa-
tion I could (which, by the way, was little if any thing at all) I
started for Washington. Having no pass I was stopped by the
Guards about half way between Camp and Alexandria. Not
being able to find the Commanding Officer I was unable to
procure one. . . . So I dismissed the carriage and after much
time and trouble succeeded in getting into a very indifferent
and uninviting Hotel. So here I am with a mighty slim pros-
pect of spending a comfortable night. . . . You have no idea of
the exorbitant prices that are charged for every thing pertaining
to Military. I will not have sufficient money, so I intend asking
Gideon to lend me fifty dollars. . . . It will be impossible for me
to do without a horse. So please think of the best way to supply
me. I am told the Regiment is constantly on the move. So you
see the difficulty I would have in accompanying it. . . . I never
saw so many niggers in all my life as are here. You see
contrabands of all sizes, ages and colors walking the streets con-
stantly. Tell the Girls to write me often and I will return the
compliment as soon as possible. Pa, you must write me as often
as convenient.[2]

The dilapidated 105th Regiment was probably represen-
tative of McClellan's whole army, which had started toward Richmond the previous April, but had never got
there. Bad weather, rebuffs by the enemy, and an overcautious commander brought it floundering back toward
Washington, depleted in numbers and equipment, after
some two months or more of ineffective campaigning.

Major General Philip S. Kearny, formerly in command of
the 1st Brigade, had been killed at Chantilly on September 1, 1862.

After one night in that uninviting hotel near Alexandria, the major, by a ruse, returned to Washington,
where presumably he managed to get himself a uniform.
On September 18 he wrote:

> *This morning I proceeded to Alexandria for the purpose of going to Washington. Arriving there I was informed that a pass from my Colonel, countersigned by the Brigade and Division Generals, was absolutely necessary to pass me to Washington. There seemed to be no other way to get out of the difficulty but to go back to camp. When there I was uncertain if I could obtain a pass—also of the time it would take. This I knew would run up a pretty large bill at the Hotel—where they charge two dollars and seventy five cents a day. So, after considering the matter, I determined to go to Alexandria and take my chances without a pass. I did it and to my great delight succeeded in smuggling myself through the Guards. I, being in civilian dress, was not noticed in the crowd entering the boat. I got here without any further difficulty. . . . I went to the war department today for a pass and transportation. The former I received—the [latter] I did not. They said a Surgeon was a Staff Officer and was supposed to have his own horse—therefore no transportation given me. . . . I go up tomorrow. Kearny's division is now commanded by Genl. Birney. It is in Heintzelman's Corps. My love to all the Girls.[3]*

After three days of shuttling in and out of Washington,
the new surgeon caught up with his regiment at Camp
Prescott, Virginia (the name was later changed to Camp

Prescott Smith), where he soon adjusted to the rugged routine. On September 20 he wrote his father:

> *This is my second night in camp. Last night I slept upon the ground in a tent without sides. Had as comfortable a night's rest as if I had been in my own bed at Home. Think I will like Camp life well—although it is a very hard life. . . . I will send my trunk home by Express as no officer is permitted to carry more than a Carpet sack. I bought a very fine overcoat and was unfortunate enough to have it stolen from me. The way it occurred was this. I hired a Carriage to bring me to camp—our Regiment having moved about a mile. I got out of the Carriage to enquire its locality. The driver went to a Sutler's wagon to get a drink of cider—and in our absence some rascal stole the coat. I can buy a common soldier's overcoat for seven dollars which will answer all purposes. I find I cannot do without a horse. The Regiment may march at any moment. I am compelled to find my own transportation. Only four wagons are allowed each Regiment. Of course I cannot ride in one of them. Even if I could, the wagons being far in the rear, I would not be able to keep up with the Regiment. The Ambulances are under the special control of an officer and are not permitted to be used for any other purpose than transporting the sick. So you perceive if the Regiment should move I would be in a bad fix—would have to foot it to keep up with the Brigade. I wish you would send me a horse to Washington as soon as possible. Get me one that will be easy kept and of sufficient age to stand hard knocks. I prefer a small horse—don't buy any thing extra—just a good ordinary horse. . . . The Assistant Surgeons are well mounted. That is, they have horses but nothing above common. . . . We occupy the most advanced fort for the defence of Washington. The first As*

*sistant graduated with me at the University. The second gradu-
ated in 1857—and is a fine fellow and a good Physician. Our
Hospital Steward is a Doctor—and has practiced nine years. I
will be very much engaged for some time in order to learn the
routine of business. The responsibilities of the entire medical
control of the Regiment rest upon the Surgeon. My love to the
Girls. Write soon.[4]*

*T*HE 105TH PENNSYLVANIA remained at Camp Prescott
about three more weeks. In his letters the youthful major, like all soldiers eager for mail, reproved the home
folks for not writing oftener, emphasized his need of a
horse, passed along rumors of military movements, and
described what he saw around camp. On September 24:

*I have no idea how long we will remain here. May move in a
day or may not for a month, though things look very much like
an advance now. A Sergeant of ordnance told me this morning
that orders were just received directing them to have ten days'
rations on hand. I only hope we shall not be ordered away until
I get my horse. Then I shall be anxious for a speedy advance. It
is imperatively necessary for a Surgeon to be with his Regiment—
and as there is not an extra horse in the whole Regt. I would
have some difficulty in keeping with the Regt. especially as I am
not a very good walker. . . . The mail is just in and I feel very
much disappointed in not hearing from home. The weather
has been very pleasant until about an hour ago when it began
to rain. But having a good tent and plenty of Blankets I defy it.
It is rather expensive living here as we buy all our provisions
from Sutlers who charge enormously for everything. We have a*

very pleasant mess Composed of myself and two Assistants. Many here suppose our Corps will advance into Va. for the purpose of cutting off the Enemy's retreat. There are about sixty or seven[ty] five thousand men in Genl. Heintzelman's Corps. Could you only see the fortifications surrounding Washington you would have no fears for its safety. Men are constantly employed on them, Sundays not excepted. Each fort is surrounded with Rifle Pits which extend to the adjacent forts. So if we should be driven out of one fort we would have the Rifle Pits to retreat to. . . . Some of these forts command the Country for miles. I have been very busy and much annoyed to day examining applicants for discharge. This is a necessary consequence of a change of Surgeons. Those who have applied before and received no certificate from the former Surgeon always besiege a new Surgeon. Some really deserve certificates. Others do not—as they are only playing sick. I have been interrupted several times since commencing this letter by fellows trying to play "old soldier." . . . Tell Miss Sue I shall take good care of the poor Rebs. Should amputation be necessary I will perform it in the most scientific manner. . . . I send my trunk home by Adams express—not being allowed to carry it. A soldier's baggage is very light. I saw it stated that the Rebels carried plenty of live stock with them. I don't think they have any advantage of us in this line—as vermin of all kinds require constant vigilance for fear of invasion. Officers are not more exempt than privates. . . . Love to Pa and the Girls. I want you all to write me often.[5]

Apprehension in Washington over possible capture of the city, and the disastrous effect of such a calamity, led to early defenses there and speeded up the building of more after the Bull Run rout of July 1861. Eventually the environs, particularly on the Virginia side, were studded with forts.

For the time being all was reasonably quiet along the Potomac while soldiers played the familiar army game of manufacturing and transmitting rumors. Major Watson got a horse, of a sort, but he need not have been disturbed by the possibility of sudden movement. General McClellan, contemplating his shaken army after the bloody Battle of Antietam on September 17, 1862, seemed indisposed to order a general advance or to use Camp Prescott troops to intercept retreating Confederates. On September 26 the major wrote:

> *You can't conceive how badly I feel when our Postmaster comes into Camp with no letters for me. Why don't I get some? . . . I am inclined to think our Post Master was drunk today. The mail arrives in Camp always about 3 o'clock P.M. Did not arrive today until after 7 o'clock P.M. It is very probable some of the letters were lost. As they were nearly all wet, I intend making it my business to report him to the Colonel tomorrow. Col. McKnight arrived last night, for which I am very sorry as he has the reputation of being very harsh and overbearing both to Officers and men. We had all hoped Lieut. Col. Craig would be made Col. . . . . Fearing our Regt. might receive marching orders and I, having no horse, would be left in the lurch, I asked Wat if he could not supply me with one. He said Tom Richardson had a captured one he would sell for thirty five dollars. I told Tom I would take him on trial for several days. . . . I must confess he is as hard a looking piece of Horseflesh as ever I backed. Still he gets over ground pretty well "Considering." This morning as I was returning to Camp mounted on my charger I met*

Doctor Pancoast, Medical Director of our division, with Genl. Birney and Staff. As we saluted I thought I could discern a humorous smirk on the faces of each one of them. I rode proudly by, however, thinking it no disgrace to ride poor horse flesh in this part of the world. Wat lent me a saddle and bridle, telling me I might forget to return them. . . . If the Horse after trial proves to be worth what Tom asks for him and as I don't have to pay cash I will keep him for my servant or orderly to ride. It would be very convenient to keep two horses. I could carry with me enough Blankets to keep me warm the coldest night, also my Clothes. . . . I am allowed forage for four horses. Forage is estimated at a dollar a month for each horse. That would amount to 32 dollars monthly. Formerly if you kept only one horse you received twenty four dollars in money. Now we are only allowed forage for horses actually kept. This of course reduces a Surgeon's pay 24 dollars a month. Therefore I can keep four horses as easy or rather as cheap as none at all. I wish you would send me a horse as soon as possible. . . . The nights are getting very cold. I bought 3 additional blankets. None are superfluous. I don't expect to be here long. I think a speedy advance will be made on Richmond. If they don't advance this fall we might as well give up the fight. What do you think of the President's Proclamation?[6]

On forage allowance, either the major's arithmetic was faulty, or he was confused about the allotment regulations. Nevertheless, after only a week as a soldier, he was learning his way around. For the moment no alarms and excursions alerted Heintzelman's 3rd Corps, which needed time to recuperate from bruising encounters in late August and early September with Robert E. Lee's versatile lieutenants, Stonewall Jackson and J. E. B. Stuart. Writing to his sister Ella on September 27, Major Watson repeated his complaint of laggard family correspondents and depicted the sprawling encampment in words that give point to Walt Whitman's "Bivouac on a Mountainside," with its "numerous camp-fires scattered near and far, some away up on the mountain"; and to "the watch-fires of a hundred circling camps" of "The Battle Hymn of the Republic":

> To day's mail in and no letter for me. I can't tell you how much I am disappointed. What is the reason I don't hear from you? . . . I have just returned from Wat's Camp. . . . He is fixed more comfortably and lives much better than I do. I took supper with him. He had soft boiled eggs and oysters. Think of that when I have not seen milk or cream, much less eggs and oysters since here. I can get plenty butter for forty cents a pound. But it is so strong that it cannot be eaten. After a while when I have more experience in catering I shall live better. I have always plenty of soft bread, meat and Coffee. That is diet sufficient for a soldier. You ought to be here at night to take a view of Distant Camp fires scattered upon the surrounding hills. It is the most magnificent sight I ever beheld. There are thousands upon thousands of fires in view. The reflection of the light of the fires by tents resembles a large city in a state of illumination. . . . The Philadelphia Zouaves are encamped just in our front. They have a splendid Band. Only one Band is allowed each Brigade—formerly there was a band to every Regiment. We have plenty of martial music, Bugles too. There are so many calls that the music is going eternally. One gets tired of so much. . . . It was reported in camp to day that Genl. Sigel had sent up from Centreville

for reinforcements and that our Corps would be sent down. Don't know if it's reliable or not. Heintzelman's Corps was so much cut up and exhausted that it is supposed it will have a pretty long rest soon to fully recruit. However, we may be thrown behind the rebels at any moment so as to cut off their retreat. I have very little to do now in the practice of medicine or Surgery. But am pretty busy preparing reports, requisitions and discharges. If we had a full Regiment I would be very busy. The drums in the whole Camp are now sounding for roll call. It is just 9 o'clock P.M. I hope you are all well at home and if you have neglected writing you will in future mend your ways. . . . I have said so much about a horse that I am ashamed to urge it any more—knowing Pa will send me one as soon as practicable. . . . Write soon. Don't forget to send the Bedford Papers.[7]

Major General Franz Sigel's 11th Corps had been at Centreville since the Union repulse at second Bull Run in late August. The report of his sending for reinforcements must have been unreliable, for the 105th Pennsylvania did not leave camp.

Writing to his father on September 29, the major was somewhat the professional practitioner, and he also apparently settled the vexing question about a horse:

I get along very well with my Assistants. I don't apprehend having any difficulty in getting along pleasantly with the Colonel and the Staff generally. The Line Officers are mostly farmers, rather rough but withal very clever. I cured one of our Captains of Chronic Diarrhea with Nitro Argent. He has been talking so much about it that I am considered a number one Physician. The former Surgeon had been treating him for several months without any benefit. . . . You need not send me a horse at present. I will try old Shellbark for a while, he may probably suit me. He is very thin—belonged to a Secesh Captain of Cavalry and of course is run down. He has sound limbs and eats well. I will see what effect rest and plenty of oats will do for him. . . . We had a grand review of our whole Brigade yesterday. The Col. ordered me to attend mounted. I told him I had no horse fit to ride. Still I had much difficulty in getting excused. There will be no help for it next time—so I have made up my mind to mount old Shellbark. . . . I am very glad the Photographs were good. Tell Miss Sue the credit of turning out my toes does not belong to me as I only occupied the position the Artist placed me in. He told me several times to turn out my toes more. There is not a particle of danger of the rebels attacking us here. We are too strongly fortified. We may remain here all winter or leave tomorrow for all I know. We have six Regiments in our Brigade now—and I can't think it possible we will remain here inactive all fall. Still our duty may be to man the forts here. . . . I am going to Alexandria tomorrow to have the Medical Purveyor fill a requisition for Hospital Supplies. I will see if I can't pick up a good Colored boy to do my cooking. I have one of the Hospital Attendants performing this work for me at present. It is pretty hard cooking, though. Then I have to eat at Hospital now and that don't suit me very well. I have by this time, with the aid of my Clerk, made myself master of all my duties. Had I gone into a full Regiment I would not have succeeded so well. Don't feel a bit uneasy about me as I will get along well.[8]

The 105th numbered less than three hundred. Regiments were seldom at full strength on either side. The major later said that the 1st Brigade—composed of the 20th

Indiana, 63rd, 68th, 105th, 114th, and 141st Pennsylvania—mustered three thousand men; thus each regiment had, on an average, about half its normal complement.

Something resembling more active duty occurred when the major's regiment went on a week's picket duty below Fairfax Court House, well south of Camp Prescott Smith. Since no Confederate pickets appeared and nobody shot anybody, this service was more like a lark than grim war. The major enjoyed his first view of a new part of Virginia, relished fresh milk and vegetables at farmhouses, gave old Shellbark a good tryout, and, in a letter of October 8, duly recorded impressions of what he called "a delightful time":

> I like my horse very much. He is just the kind for military service. The only objection to him is his extreme laziness. Don't mind the spur hardly a bit. I intend buying a pair of Mexican spurs when I think he will do better. . . . When on picket I stopped at the house of a Lady named Surrett. She has been living some years in Washington. Is a Virginian by birth. Is very intelligent. Her husband was a soldier in the war of 1812. Had a son in the Regular Army who was killed in Mexico. Had another son in the Navy—he was drowned. Says she is a good Unionist. But wants the Constitution and Union as it was and as Washington and his Compeers made it. She lives only a few miles from Bull Run battle ground. After the battle in July '61 she said the heavens were overcast with black clouds and the rain poured down in torrents. Said it was God hiding his face and weeping over the wickedness of his children. The old Lady's daughter in law is living with her. I thought she was a widow— but have since learned that her husband is in the southern Army.

From many things both of them said I could easily see their sympathies were all with the rebels. . . . Suppose there will be no draft in Pa. as the Gov. is given his own time to provide Pa. quota. This of course will render easy the mind of some of my old Bedford Co. friends. . . . The Officers and men all say that Col. McKnight has changed very much. He is much more lenient than before. He has gotten rid of three or four obnoxious Officers since his return. It is supposed he will now rest easy.[9]

There may be irony in that reference to "old Bedford Co. friends," some of whom, living cushioned lives at home, may have stirred the major's disdain by their eagerness to avoid the draft. In camp rumors flew: of provision wagons assigned to the brigade preparatory to an immediate march to join McClellan in Maryland, or to advance with Sigel into enemy country. Major Watson hoped for a big push against Richmond and its capture before winter. But nothing much happened except that his father forwarded a horse, which, after 150 miles of travel in four days, arrived the worse for wear. Furthermore, the major, apprised of possible trouble for himself, reversed his opinion of Colonel McKnight's change for the better; in a second letter on October 8 he told a story of internal regimental friction, real and potential:

A great friend of mine, Captain Markle, came to me yesterday. He thought it was his duty to put me on guard against the Colonel. Says he is a great friend of Dr. Heichold, the former Surgeon of this Regiment. The Doctor resigned in a pet—and is very anxious to return again to the Regt. The Colonel desires the same result. The Captain said the Colonel was a very dishonorable and treacherous scamp and would take the first opportunity to prefer charges against me and have me dismissed. I can't believe he is such a rogue. So far he has treated me with great kindness and Courtesy. Don't think he would take any such advantage of me. Still I intend to attend closely to my duties and obey all his Commands that are in accordance with law and the Regulations. Therefore I have no fears of any thing unpleasant occurring between himself and me. Should I find any difficulty in getting along with him I will apply to be transferred to another Regiment. Have no such fears, however. Time enough to complain when injured. . . . Lost a patient in hospital yesterday. Was sick only twenty four hours. Died of Congestion of the Brain. Have in Hospital 19 patients. Four of these I intend having discharged as they will never be fit for service. The Colonel has preferred charges against major Greenewalt for cowardice. It is supposed he will be dismissed. It is a great shame. He is a very nice fellow and as far as I can ascertain did not exhibit any cowardice. The charges were brought by the Adjutant, a great friend of the Col.'s at the Col.'s instigation. Three Lieutenants have handed in their resignations in the last few days. That indicates beyond doubt the unpopularity of the Colonel. The Quartermaster has also resigned. Their places will doubtless be filled with the friends of the Colonel. . . . Troops are constantly leaving for Maryland to join McClellan. Camps filled with Regiments a few days ago are now entirely deserted. I[t] looks very much to me that our Corps will be left to defend the fortifications. Should this be the case I will have an easy time this winter.[10]

Idiosyncrasies of commanders, jealousies, and maneuvering for preferment hampered the Army of the Potomac, to the disadvantage of soldiers who did the fighting. They paid the price exacted by blundering leaders who were only politicians in uniform—though this cannot be said of Colonel McKnight, who, in action, became an inspiring commander. It is interesting to note, however, that similar personality crotchets and internal bickering also plagued Confederate armies. Major (then Captain) Greenewalt, cited by McKnight for meritorious service at Yorktown on May 4, 1862, had been wounded at Fair Oaks, May 31. The alleged "cowardice" was possibly a figment of the testy colonel's imagination. The major's low hospital statistics show that he was a good medical officer; the 105th Regiment had less sickness than any other in the division.

In a few days the 1st Brigade marched out of camp: to Rockville, Maryland, then to Poolesville, Conrad's Ferry, and back to Poolesville again, slogging forty-five miles in two days through a steady downpour. Major Watson was proud to report that his regiment had no stragglers; whereas when the fancy Philadelphia Zouaves reached Conrad's Ferry, half their number had wilted by the wayside en route. "The Boys say," remarked the major on October 13,

> it was the hardest work in that line they have ever had. They are, as you know, old veterans and understand campaigning. We had awful weather. Rained all the time. Our object in coming here was to intercept the rebels who had been in Pa. We reached Conrad's ferry about four hours after the rebels had crossed. There were twenty eight hundred rebels. We had three thousand Infantry—all Robinson's Brigade and some Cavalry. We certainly expected a sharp fight. The Boys are all eager for it. I am very sorry we were not up in time. The rebels must have

*carried off a great many horses. We had no tents with us. So we
slept on the ground. I would not [have] thought any person
could have slept so comfortably on the wet ground with the
rain beating down in his face. . . . I am sitting on the ground
writing on my knee. Don't know how long we will remain
here—will probably move this morning.*[11]

The retreating Confederates were part of the cavalry of
General Stuart returning from an extensive foray before
and after the Battle of Antietam. In this campaign
Stuart's horsemen had ridden entirely around the army
of General McClellan, collecting many horses on the way,
and after the battle had descended upon Chambersburg,
Pennsylvania, where they appropriated government
equipment and destroyed great quantities they could not
carry with them. General Alfred Pleasonton, with a small
force of Union cavalry, harassed the invaders' rear, but
they got back across the Potomac without serious trouble.
This ride of Stuart's cavalry was one of the most spectacular exploits of that brilliant commander.

Major Watson, chagrined at not being "up in time"
to intercept, remarked upon one of those bungled op-
portunities that, in the Army of the Potomac, often nul-
lified an advantage, failed to follow up a victory, or frustrated a bold tactic. Still, his own morale was unquenched
by rain or disappointment; though a newcomer to campaigning, he seemed an able comrade of those veterans
he had praised. "It is said," he observed in another letter
on October 13,

*the 99th Pa. Regt., nearly a thousand strong, permitted them to
cross without firing a shot. If they had held them for several*

hours—and they could have done it without any trouble—our Brigade would have reinforced them and the whole of Stuart's Cavalry would have been defeated if not captured. . . . If my information is correct the rebels' escape is entirely owing to the cowardly and dastardly conduct of the 99th Pa. Our Regt., though only numbering two hundred and fifty, is considered the star Regt. in the Brigade. Genl. Robinson always places it in the advance. Dear Pa, I assure you a soldier's life in time of war is not one of ease and comfort. During the whole march we were in a drenching rain. Our rations consist in Crackers and Pork. I generally go to a farm house when one is in sight at meal time. When a halt or rest is ordered the Boys throw themselves on the wet ground and sleep as comfortably as if in a tent or house and apparently without any disagreeable consequences to themselves. My horse suits admirably for marching. He walks just about fast enough to keep up and no faster. Was offered one hundred and twenty five dollars for him this morning. The Colonel thinks we will go to Leesburg tonight. But don't anticipate meeting any of the enemy there. There is no doubt but we will have a very active fall campaign. The rebels certainly deserve great credit for the successful raid into and retreat from our state. Suppose you were all considerably alarmed at their being so near. The troops here put a low estimate upon our Cavalry. The rebel Cavalry is certainly more efficient than ours. . . . Let the Girls write me very often. . . . Please don't forget the Bedford papers.[12]

The surmise that enemy cavalry might have been defeated or captured was probably overoptimistic. The elusive Stuart was not easily cornered. Many places in southern Pennsylvania were alarmed by Lee's invasion. At

Antietam, or Sharpsburg, Maryland, the Army of Northern Virginia, including the corps of the fearsome Jackson, had been within about forty miles of Bedford, and Stuart's raiders may have been closer. The major's comment on cavalry is apt. Not until near the end of the war, when Confederate cavalry was weakened by losses and a scarcity of good mounts, did Union horsemen, armed with better weapons than their opponents, become a fair match. Even then the swashbuckling Federal commander, General Philip Sheridan, was not as efficient in gathering information about enemy movements as Stuart had been for Lee.

Major Watson's expectations of an active fall campaign did not materialize, McClellan being afflicted with what Lincoln called "the slows." The 1st Brigade of the 3rd Corps, including the 105th Pennsylvania, remained in camp near Poolesville, Maryland, until late October, making occasional marches but not colliding with the enemy. The major, writing home often, admitted that he seemed to have become "exceedingly fond of letter writing." Although he wrote hurriedly at odd moments— sometimes scratching a blurry note while sitting propped against a tree—his perception illuminated his missives with a variety of detail. On October 15 he said:

> *Yesterday morning at 3 o'clock we left Camp and marched to the Mouth of the Monocacy, a distance of 12 miles. We did picket duty there until 1 o'clock last night. Being relieved by an other Regt. we returned to Camp—making in all a march of 24 miles. The Boys, being very anxious to get home to the warm blankets and tents and also hungry, went the last five miles in an hour. I*

had the pleasure of eating only one meal in twenty four hours. But fared better than my horse who had nothing. The rebels did not cross, as I before stated, at Conrad's but at White's ferry which is several miles above the former. They had with them nearly a thousand Horses captured in Pa. I regret so much our Brigade did not succeed in intercepting them. They would certainly have had to disgorge this booty. I breakfasted this morning in a farm house near Camp. It was decidedly Secesh. One of the Girls remarked that in her opinion the Southern soldiers were much braver than the Northern. Had she been a man I would certainly have given the lie to it in no very polite or gentle manner. But as it was I passed it without notice and left without further conversation. But not until I had eaten my breakfast. This is a strong Secesh County. I saw it stated in a Baltimore paper that it sent but seven volunteers. When at the Monocacy we were distant only six miles from seventeen thousand rebels. Having but four thousand we did not care to get much nearer. Our force was sufficient, however, to prevent them crossing the river. Berry's and Birney's Brigades are now here and with ours constitute Stoneman's division. Genl. Stoneman is here. . . . I felt particularly good when marching towards old Pennsylvania. I am going to Poolesville this morning for oats. The Quarter Master will not have any till tomorrow and my horse has been without feed for thirty six hours. . . . Ella asks me if I am homesick. Tell her not in the least, although I should like nothing in the world better than to see all. . . . To day we hold an election in Camp. It is going on very quietly, the Boys seeming to take very little interest in it. I intend voting only the state and Congressional tickets. I hope you will send me the Bedford papers every week. . . . I like to read the Army Correspondence in it—so I will know if I am near any of our Bedford Boys.[13]

*F*OUR DAYS LATER, on October 19, he wrote again:

> *I like the Army very much—although it is a very hard life. Few a[t] home have any idea of a soldier's hardships and privations. A few nights ago we moved our Camp a short distance. I neglected having a drain dug around my tent. I woke up in the morning completely saturated with rain. I had four blankets, they were wet through as well as my underclothes. But I am happy to say I experienced no unpleasant effects from my ducking. We are encamped near the Potomac and are here for the purpose of guarding Conrad's, Noland's, Edwards and White's ferrys and preventing further raids into Maryland and Pennsylvania. Are four miles from Leesburg. We were fortunate, when pursuing Stuart after his Pa. raid, in not crossing the river. Stuart received heavy reinforcements at Leesburg and waited for us to come up. Had we gone it would have been another Ball's bluff affair. . . . This is a great Country for "Chills and fever." Hope I will escape as the Camp is the worst place in the world for a sick person. I never enjoyed better health in my life. Please write often. The other Girls must do likewise. Also send me the Bedford papers regularly.*[14]

Ball's Bluff, Virginia, near Leesburg, was the scene of a Union rout on October 21, 1861, when one battery and parts of four regiments were pushed over the cliff into the Potomac River, and acting Brigadier General E. D. Baker, a close friend of Lincoln's, was killed. Another casualty was the late Justice of the United States Supreme Court, then Lieutenant Oliver Wendell Holmes, 20th Massachusetts. In the bitter aftermath of this defeat, hotheaded editors accused the division commander,

General Charles P. Stone, of treason. The notorious Committee on the Conduct of the War besmirched the reputations of officers in Baker's "California Regiment" and imprisoned Stone for months without formally preferring charges or ever bringing him to trial. Even McClellan was suspected of treason. The Ball's Bluff episode is a vivid illustration of tense times when hysterical emotion overrode good sense.

The major's pride in abounding health was premature, for in this chills-and-fever country he was laid low by what he called "something like Bilious Remittent fever." Yet his sturdy spirit was not depressed as he gaily described his rough-hewn sleeping quarters. "You just ought to see my bed," he wrote on October 23:

> It is composed of two fence rails with flour barrel staves nailed to them. This is elevated about six inches from the ground, being set on two boards. I have one gum and two woolen blankets under me and two above me. This, with my clothes for a pillow, constitutes my bed. But I sleep as comfortably in this rude bed as I [ever] did in my life. I wrote Pa a few days ago to send me some little money. I am in great need of some at present, having spent all for a few little delicacies since sick. I will tell you what a few things cost—so you will have an idea of the enormous prices demanded for everything. Butter sells at forty cents a pound. Eggs 25 cts. a doz. Spring chickens one dollar a pair. Most of the time you can't get any of them at all. Officers, of course, board themselves and must have money to do so. I live very plainly and economically, generally having nothing but Bacon, bread without butter, and Coffee. I pray God I may hear soon from home.[15]

$\mathscr{A}$FTER TREATING HIMSELF, he was on his feet again in about a week, somewhat groggy, yet shrugging off the fever that was, he said, "a very common affair in this miasmatic country." Continual rain, hampering military movements, made him take a dim view of the Maryland locality, and perhaps inspired caustic comments on stay-at-home strategists who offered gratuitous advice on the proper way to win the war. "This is a most miserable Secesh hole," he wrote on October 26,

> and one is no safer here when riding outside the lines than in Virginia. There are plenty of scamps here willing and ready to put a bullet through a "Yankee soldier" any time, could they do it in safety. . . . The news papers think the Army should take Richmond before going into Winter Quarters. On marches it is impracticable for soldiers to carry their tents with them. They are transported in wagons—which are always in the rear. Even if the wagons were with the soldiers it would not pay to unload and strike tents for a rest of a few hours. Hence mother earth and the open Canopy of heaven constitute both bed and tent for the weary soldier. How absurd then to talk of an active campaign in the winter. It is physically impossible. Let those erudite editors who are continually crying out against Winter Quarters experience in person an active winter campaign and see how soon they would counsel going into those very Winter Quarters they are now condemning. Dr. Vollum, Med. Inspector U.S.A., paid me a visit yesterday. He desired me to write out the Medical History of our Regt. I informed him I was just appointed to the Regt., that the Surgeon and Assistant Surgeon had both resigned, leaving no data by which the nature and treat[ment] of disease could be ascertained and that consequently

that I could not do it. He said I should ascertain any facts concerning epidemics that had prevailed and report them. As it is a positive order from the Surgeon Genl. I will have to comply and furnish the best Medical History possible. I promise you it will be a short one.[16]

Editors freely offered advice on the conduct of the war, and some of them, copperheads and antiwar Democrats, bitterly denounced it. One of the most articulate Union spokesmen was Horace Greeley, of the influential New York *Tribune*. He was a well-meaning worrier and a nagging alarmist and became such a trial to Lincoln that in a famous letter to the editor on August 22, 1862, the president attempted to clarify his policy by stating that his purpose was to save the Union regardless of what he did about slavery.

The major, expecting a move any moment and still shaky enough to be dubious about staying on a horse, bethought himself of riding in an ambulance. In another letter of October 26 he said:

I can take a seat in one and follow the Regt. as comfortably as any one could desire. In fact, I would rather be in one of them on a rainy day than in a tent. The Ambulances are formed into a Corps commanded by a Lieutenant. Each Regt. is allowed, according to the Regulations, two four and ten two-wheeled ones. Our Regt. has the two former and but one of the latter. They are subject to my order—so I will ride in one of them till the weather changes for the better. My horse "Crow" is doing finely. But is as lazy as ever. I sold old "Shellbark" for the same I gave for him. Did not get the money but a note that will be cashed on pay day. I have some very good Hospital Attendants. Two of them are

*devoted to me. One of them was by my side anticipating my
every wish the entire time I was sick. The Regiment, I believe,
likes me better than the former Surgeon—at least as good. Many
of them tell me so. It still rains—and it is very uncomfortable
in tents without fire.*[17]

The two-wheeled ambulance was a fiendish contraption.
An unstable vehicle, it turned every slight jog into a jolt
that aggravated the misery of sick and wounded men.
Apropos of the note to be "cashed on pay day," nobody
in this camp had seen any pay since the major had joined
the regiment six weeks before. In late October, General
George Stoneman's division moved a few miles upriver,
then crossed the Potomac to make camp near Leesburg,
Virginia. Since the ambulances of the 105th were filled
with sick, the major said, "I could not find it in my heart
to ride and let them walk." He rode his horse, after all,
and slept on the ground—in the rain, as usual, this latest of several duckings making him, he believed,
"weather proof." From the new camp he wrote on October 30:

*Our whole division is on the Va. side of the Potomac. We crossed
without resistance from the rebels. Having no bridge the Boys
waded the river. It was pretty cold work—but they did it without a murmur. We don't know how soon we may have a fight.
. . . We are now encamped on Ball's Bluff. But have no fears of
that sad Catastrophe being repeated. If they have evacuated Winchester I only trust we will rapidly be pushed after them so as to
harass and do them as much mischief as possible. They never
permit us to retreat without molestation—a thing very common, however, with us. . . . Present appearances indicate an*

active Winter Campaign. Should this be the case we will have a very rough time this Winter. I can stand it if others can. Active campaigning in pleasant weather is certainly more agreeable than inactive Camp life. The same old routine day after day is a great bore. Still I think it preferable to long and fatiguing marches and all the hardships incident to active duty in field in the winter months. At present the weather is delightful. It must be Indian Summer. There are thousands of partridges here. You see them in almost any direction. And it being such a pleasant country to shoot in—it is not surprising I often wish for Jack and the Gun. . . . The Boys have killed all the Chickens and Pigs in the neighborhood. This thing of guarding Secesh property is about "played out." I for one consider it lawful and perfectly proper to appropriate any thing in the shape of feed and forage I can lay my hand on. If you desire to buy any thing, five or six prices are asked. The only trouble is there is little or nothing to appropriate. Virginia is pretty well eaten up. Near our present Camp there were three large stacks of wheat. In twenty four hours there was not one sheaf left. It was used as beds for the Boys and feed for the Horses. The fences were all good when we arrived. Now not one rail is visible as far as the eye can reach.[18]

The quick disappearance of food on the hoof, wheat, and fence rails highlights the havoc wrought by an invading army. After eighteen months of war, Virginia had been fought over, trampled, and ravaged—and would be for more than two years longer.

The 105th Pennsylvania remained near Leesburg until early November, making sporadic marches and enlivening camp monotony with customary rumors and conjectures. Major Watson observed, reported events that interested him, speculated, and delivered himself of opinions military and political. "The new Regiments in our Brigade," he said on October 31,

> *are very anxious for the fray. Not so with the war worn veterans of the 105th. They, having been engaged in many desperate and sanguinary battles, are not particularly eager for the reenactment of those bloody scenes. They don't fear battle. When it comes they take it as a matter of course and will stand to their work more bravely than the men who so anxiously desire fight. They know full well battle implies the loss of many a dear friend and comrade. Hence they (as the papers say) are not "spoiling for a fight." Leesburg is a very pretty town. Contains about two thousand inhabitants. The doors and windows were crowded with persons (mostly females). But the only demonstrations that greeted us were sullen looks and scornful expressions. These were unheeded as we marched through in stern and contemptuous silence. I don't believe one person favorable to the Union can be found in this part of Virginia. You can't conceive how indignant I feel at the result of the Pa. election. It proves beyond the peradventure of a doubt that the great Union army contains many more Republicans than Democrats. Certainly no one deprecates the defeat of the Union party throughout the whole North [more] than myself. I know there are a great many good loyal war democrats elected. But I fear the majority are "dough faces" or in other words Southern sympathizers. . . . I like my present situation very well. Would not be satisfied any place else just now.[19]*

The 1862 elections, which had gone heavily against the Republicans, were generally interpreted as a vote of no confidence in Lincoln's administration. Both Senate and House gained Democratic members. New York, Ohio, Pennsylvania, Indiana, and Illinois—all of which had polled Republican majorities in 1860—sent Democratic majorities to Congress in 1862. To many Unionists, Lincoln's policy seemed vacillating and timid. He was beset not only by an adroit military enemy poorly opposed by his own stumbling generals, but also, on the home front, by abolitionists, copperheads, peace Democrats, radical and moderate Republicans, importunate editors, and would-be subversives like the Knights of the Golden Circle, Knights of the Columbian Star, and other undercover groups hoping to touch off melodramatic terrorism. Truly, as Walt Whitman wrote a few months later, Lincoln showed "an almost supernatural tact in keeping the ship afloat at all, with head steady, not only not going down, and now certain not to, but with proud and resolute spirit, and flag flying in sight of the world, menacing and high as ever. I say never yet captain, never ruler, had such a perplexing dangerous task as his, the past two years."

Next day, November 1, the major wrote again:

I visited Leesburg this morning for the purpose of procuring some provisions. After some difficulty I secured two loaves of bread. They were very small but cost twenty five cents each. The old Dutchman from whom I purchased them said there were only two Union families in the town. That information was an agreeable surprise—as I was under the impression there was not one family in the whole Country. Just as I was entering Camp I encountered a wagon loaded with apple pies—and mighty common ones they were. I bought two for forty cents. Still I was perfectly satisfied with my morning's mission, having procured sufficient to make a comfortable, if not sumptuous, dinner. In town I met a rebel Surgeon who, prior to the war, resided in Leesburg. He said he had a brace of fine dogs and if it were not contrary to orders would give me a fine day's shooting. I thanked him kindly—but told him I feared the rebel "Bushwhackers" would bag me before I succeeded in bagging many birds. There has been very heavy and rapid cannonading the past few hours in the direction of Ashby's Gap. It still continues, report after report in rapid succession. If the Rebels remain in their present position I think the greatest battle of the war will soon be fought. God grant the Union army may triumph. Elly in her letter says she fears I will not be able to stand Camp life and advises me not to expose myself "at all." Pretty advice to a soldier. I shall, as I said before, not recklessly expose myself for I value life as much as any one. But it shall never be said that I shirked duty to avoid danger. . . . As for not being able to stand Camp life I can conscientiously say few men are better constitutionally adapted for the endurance of hardships than myself. . . . [My Philadelphia friends] will acquire easy manners and polite address while this poor Boy, associating with rough but brave and true hearted men, will lose all the little polish he ever possessed and when he again makes his debut in fashionable society will rival old Bruin himself in manners. But so goes the world. I received the Bedford Gazette you sent. It is a vile sheet. One of the Boys read it and remarked he would like to hang the Editor. . . . The Quarter Master just came into my tent and said, "Well, Doctor, those guns out front there have commenced to sound rather wicked." They certainly are becoming more distinct. I hope our forces are not falling back. If they do, however, they will have a strong and willing division to reinforce them. Our Army will never be driven out of Virginia again. . . . My Hospital Steward, who is also a Doctor, has his wife here. She is a good soldier. Takes every thing as it comes without exhibiting either fear or fatigue. I always give her a permit to ride in an Ambulance. She undergoes all the hardships of a soldier except picket and guard duty and walking. In fact, she is a jewel of a woman. She mended my coat for me. Tell Elly I want my back rubbed with Chloroform Linament.[20]

Since Bedford was not far from the Maryland line, possibly the editor of the *Gazette* was tinged with the secessionism that made the border state a problem for the Federal administration. The ominous cannonading was not the prelude to a great battle, and the 3rd Corps was not called out as reinforcements.

After a few days at Leesburg, however, the major's division moved some thirty-five miles southwest to Warrenton, where it became a reserve for General Pleasonton's cavalry, which had been skirmishing with Stuart's roving riders. The new camp of the 105th Regiment was on Carter's Mountain in the Blue Ridge range. "This is a wild country," wrote Major Watson on November 9:

The Blue Ridge with its lofty and at present snow clad peaks leave our old Allegheny somewhat in the shade. Though more grand in appearance it does not excite in me the same joyful and enthusiastic emotions as the blue outline of my native portion of the great chief of Pennsylvania mountains. I have not been able to decide yet which mountain blows the coldest winds. . . . The past few mornings ice from ⅛ to ¼ inch was found on buckets and basins left standing out. I have slept well during these cold nights, having plenty of bed fellows and blankets. Capt. Conser and Ewing sleep with me. By combining our stock of blankets we make a snug bed. I take the middle and consequently get very much crowded. But as one gets more heat in the middle I stand the squeezing. Yesterday and today my tent afforded fire. The tent of Dr. Crawford, my Hospital Steward, was left in Leesburg—and as he has his wife with him he was in rather an unenviable situation. I tendered him part of my tent which was willingly accepted—he, having a stove, we put it up and for two days have had the most comfortable tent in Camp. . . . I always sleep on the ground on the march as it don't pay to prepare a bunk only to occupy it one night. This is a poor country for forage, very little grain of any kind having been put in—and all that was grown has already been consumed. "Crow" don't fare so well as a week ago. I load him pretty heavily on a march—as I carry my own provisions and three blankets. I have been living, with the exception of today, on soldiers' fare—consisting of "Hard tack, Speck Sugar and Coffee." To day I dined on Corn Cakes and bean soup. . . . Rebel prisoners are constantly passing towards Warrenton. They are illy clad. I have seen but one having on an overcoat—and that was captured from Uncle Sam. . . . It is more than a week since we received our mail—but as we have such a miserable post-master I don't know when I shall hear from home or get this letter off. Our Post Master left us at Leesburg last Sunday and nothing has been heard of him since. From his antecedents the great probability is that he is drunk in Washington. . . . Two or three Corps of McClellan's Army are in the immediate vicinity. Porter's Corps, including the Pa. Reserves, passed through Middleburg the same time we did. I have no idea how the Campaign will be conducted but I think the force about here is for taking possession and holding the Gap of the Blue Ridge or getting into the rear of the Enemy and the Shenandoah Valley and preventing retreat to Richmond while McClellan attacks in front. If they are still about Winchester with their whole Army they will be in a bad fix. Dr. Ewing . . . says an old Farmer told him this county only cast four votes for the Union. . . . We are distant six miles from Warrenton and 15 or 20 from Front Royal. I only hope we may get into the rebels' rear and use them up. I believe the intention is to take Richmond, if possible, this or next month.[21]

Whatever the intentions of General McClellan, they were now of no consequence, for even as the major wrote, McClellan was no longer commander of the Army of the Potomac. His dawdling reluctance to pursue retreating Confederates after the Battle of Antietam exasperated even the patient Lincoln, who deposed the commander on November 5. His successor, Major General Ambrose E. Burnside, assumed command on November 9—the third general of this army in some fifteen months. News of these changes had evidently not reached the camp of the 105th when Major Watson wrote on November 10:

This afternoon we leave this place for either Front Royal or Culpeper. The latter is but 10 miles distant. We do not contemplate marching either place without resistance. The Rebel pickets are just opposite over the river. They are said to be at Culpeper in force. For my part I am anxious to meet them. These mountains are filled with troops. Certainly we are on the eve of a great battle. Where and when it will be fought I am unable even to conjecture. The Brigade Commissary just informed me Stuart's Cavalry had captured part of Genl. Berry's trains at

White Plains—and also taken Leesburg. Should this prove true some of our men have been taken prisoner—as a large Division Hospital was established there. I left some twenty sick there. The charge of the Hospital was offered me. I should have been there had I had some money. The town was entirely Secesh and I did not like the idea of remaining there without money—as I am obliged to supply my own provisions. I got out of it by stating my recent illness and pleading physical disability. The capture of the train, if correct, is nothing but an old and often repeated song. When will our Genls. so direct their movements as to prevent these disastrous and disgraceful occurrences?[22]

The regiment belied the major's expectations by not going anywhere for a while; no great battle ensued. His question about ineffectual generals was one that Lincoln had also asked as he searched for a commander who could lead this army. Nevertheless, Major Watson adopted a pragmatic hopefulness of better things to come. "We are in the midst of Mountains," he wrote on November 13:

It is the roughest Country I ever saw. It is just the country for one or the other party to be out generaled. It remains to be seen which will be the unfortunate party. The removal of Genl. McClellan created much surprise but no undue excitement. The common soldiers violently denounce his enemies—saying every thing now indicates a speedy and disastrous defeat. But I am sorry to say most of the Officers approve his removal. I deprecate his downfall as much as any one. Still I think with Genl. Burnside as Commander, associated with Heintzelman, Hooker, Sigel and Sumner, we have nothing to fear. . . . I have not slept in a tent for three nights. When I return home and engage in a hunting or fishing expedition it will be immaterial to me whether I sleep in a house or on the ground. You have no idea what men can stand. They can sleep on the wet ground without any cover except a blanket or two in the most disagreeable weather without any seeming inconvenience. I have been well tried and not found wanting—as I have now experienced one of the roughest and most fatiguing Campaigns imaginable. . . . We have not been paid yet. But expect to be in a few days. Then I will be able to buy myself a good warm suit—which I greatly need.[23]

The dashing ways of Major General McClellan had made him popular with troops. Yet, though exercising great talent for organization, he lacked drive and boldness in the field. At Antietam, informed by a lucky chance of the enemy's plans, he did not act promptly on this information. Outnumbering the enemy, he was fought to a standstill by Jackson and James Longstreet. McClellan, throwing his army piecemeal into uncoordinated attacks, did not even use all his reserve power and thus gained little more than a drawn battle when he might have crushed the Army of Northern Virginia. Furthermore, when the Confederates retreated, he did not follow up.

Major Watson's faith in the new commander and his associates was to prove ill-founded. The men in the ranks, growling as always, were more shrewd in their gloomy prediction of "a speedy and disastrous defeat." Poor leadership and too many setbacks had made them pessimists. The major himself admitted that "since the disorganization of Heintzelman's old Corps, composed of Hooker's and Kearny's divisions, our Boys have little confidence in any one General. If Burnside will ride around among the troops and gain one decided victory he will get the confidence of the entire Army."[24] The riding among the troops recalls McClellan's flashy habit of galloping through a camp, waving his hat while soldiers cheered; in Washington he staged a great show of urgency by clattering pell-mell through the streets, his staff pounding along behind. "Little Mac" aroused noisy enthusiasm by these spirited displays, but there was little spirit in his timid generalship during a campaign. Whether Burnside would do better was a moot question. He began to move his army to the vicinity of Fredericksburg, Virginia, for a major offensive against the well-fortified town.

*B*Y LATE NOVEMBER the 105th Pennsylvania was encamped on the north side of the Rappahannock River, within two miles of the city. In the lull of forces gathering before the storm, Major Watson dispatched a number of long letters. On November 24 he wrote:

> *The Rebels are on the other side of the Rappahannock. Their Pickets as well as ours extend to the river on either side. I went down to the River yesterday—and their pickets were distinctly visible. They converse very freely with our pickets and no shots have as yet been exchanged. Both parties, I believe, heartily disapprove pickets firing. . . . Genl. Burnside passed here yesterday evening. I like his looks well. Judging from his appearance I don't think this Army will long remain inactive. The rebels, it seems, are determined not to evacuate Fredericksburg with out [a] struggle. So the Ball may commence at any moment. Burnside, I think, is delayed by scarcity of supplies. . . . When these*

are obtained the rebels will be compelled to skedaddle. Any morning I look for the commencement of shelling the town. All the inhabitants have left, leaving it occupied only by soldiers. Our Regt. is about being consolidated—12 or 15 line Officers will be mustered out. I regret this very much—as my most particular friends are included in the fatal list. We will probably get five new companies from the drafted militia, they being permitted to officer their own companies. . . . You complain of the scarcity of Beaux. You don't seem to think that Girls are almost as indispensable as young Gentlemen. Here where we very rarely see an agreeable female face—we mourn the absence of our Lady friends fully as much as you do the Boys. How I should like once more to meet [in] Bedford the pretty Bedford Girls I should see at one of our old fashioned sociables—and reenact some of the good old times—and hear Barclay, when I had a plate of good things before me, amusing the Girls by relating my enormous feeding propensities. Here I have not seen Bread, butter or Milk for weeks—much less a nice sweet Pennsylvania Girl. . . . Tell Pa we have not been paid yet. But expect to be in a week or so. I will only get a month and half pay. Still I will be able to send, as the Virginians say, "right smart" home.[25]

The sociability of hostile pickets has been preserved by Matthew Brady, the persistent photographer who followed the Army of the Potomac. When he aimed his camera at Confederates across the Rappahannock, they posed obligingly for a group picture that suggests all the amenities of an old home week.

The major had still received no pay after more than two months in the army. This dilatoriness, typical of haphazard procedures in 1862, caused loud grumbling in the ranks. The Boston *Journal* underlined this discontent in the story of a paymaster who called at the White House because, he said, he wanted to pay his respects. Lincoln remarked: "From the complaints of soldiers, I guess that's about all any of you do pay." It is pleasant to observe the serious-minded young major thinking of girls, and savoring in his imagination the good food at those old-fashioned sociables. Soldiers of all times and all armies have much in common. But the stir of preparation on his immediate front interested him too. "Last night," he wrote on November 26,

> *I distinctly heard the town clock strike. During the day there is apparently no activity in the Burg. But all night long we hear the rattle of Cars and the scream of the Locomotive. Their intrenchments nightly grow larger. I now believe they will not evacuate without a severe fight. I have no doubt they are constantly receiving heavy reinforcements every night. Burnside's delay is attributed to want of subsistence. This is merely conjecture—as he may not intend crossing the river at this point. Our troops would sooner fight here than nearer Richmond—as the character of the ground would cause it to be almost entirely an Artillery contest. It is now rumored that Burnside will approach Richmond by the Peninsula. The river is said to be lined with transports. . . . You at the North know more about Army movements than we do as we rarely receive the papers and therefore know nothing beyond the movements of our respective Divisions and Corps. I am very busy at present, Dr. Ewing and Wenger both being under arrest . . . for not attending Division Review. . . . Tomorrow is Thanksgiving Day. It is needless to say how I should like to be with you and lend my feeble assistance*

to the consumption of our usual Thanksgiving day Turkey. Our Mess consists of four—Capt. Conser, Dr. Ewing and Wenger, and myself. I am sorry to say that, unfortunately for me, they are all good feeders. This, however, is nothing but my usual luck, as I have always, much to my own disadvantage, messed with big eaters.[26]

The chief items of Burnside's "subsistence" were pontoons to bridge the river. Because of some failure of coordination, they did not arrive for two or three weeks, while Union forces sat down, inactive, before Fredericksburg. As Major Watson surmised, the enemy took advantage of this delay to bring up reinforcements by railroad, and strongly to fortify Marye's Heights behind the town. The comment on war news in the press is a reminder of days when scarcely anything was top secret. Lax surveillance of military information permitted correspondents to publish full accounts of army movements, made and contemplated. Confederate commanders were said to have quipped that a perusal of war dispatches in New York dailies made spying unnecessary. The major, knowing nothing of grand strategy, could only speculate. On November 28 he wrote at some length:

Here we are still, having as yet made no hostile demonstration on the doomed city. And here in all probability we will long remain, if the prevalent rumor that an armistice of thirty days has been granted the rebels is correct. This information came yesterday from one of Genl. Robinson's aides. If an Armistice has really been established the President had better disband the Army at once. The rebels are in a tighter place than ever before and if we are going to let this good opportunity of demolishing them slip us we had better give up the struggle. I can't believe this rumor although coming from reliable authority. Honest old Abe would certainly not be guilty of such consummate folly. Should it prove true I shall feel greatly like throwing up my Commission and returning home and enjoying life "in otium c dignitate." . . . Drs. Ewing and Wenger are still under arrest— and as the Colonel has preferred charges against them for disobedience of orders they will be Court Martialed. The Court may not convene for a month or six weeks and, they being permitted to do no official duty, the whole onus of the Medical department will devolve on me. . . . Yesterday being Thanksgiving day I was determined to have something extra for dinner. So I went to Falmouth for the purpose of finding something in the edible line. Was very successful—securing two chickens and 4 doz. biscuits. This completely strapped me—as I had but two dollars. . . . Dr. Wenger, being rather flush, has sustained the entire expense of our Mess ever since his arrival and I only hope he may still have enough to stave off starvation till the Paymaster comes. On my way to Falmouth I rode down to the river to take an other look at Fredericksburg. . . . The pickets are near enough to engage in a stone fight. Fredericksburg is just on the river edge. Looking over, not a Woman or child is to be seen—but plenty of Graybacks come within range of one's observation. It looks strange to see squads of hostile men not fifty yards apart lounging carelessly about idly contemplating one an other. Picket talking has been interdicted—so they sit all day idly surveying each other. . . . The days and nights for the past week have been uncomfortably cold. There was no chance of buying a stove— and had there been it would have been all the same to us as we had no money to purchase one. So we put our heads together. You remember the old saying "Two heads are better than one if one is a pumpkin." I quote this in order that you, though fully aware that I am no great mechanical genius, will give me some credit in devising this novel apparatus. Having cut some pine logs and collected some mud from the road we began its construction by piling log upon log, forming an open pen—the open side extending into the tent. The crevices were then filled with mud. Having built this almost as high as the tent—we topped it off with a barrel to act as a chimney. The inside was then roughly but liberally smeared with nature's mortar. The tent was then drawn closely around the fire place to exclude the cold air. A fire was kindled and to our great delight burned vigorously and cheerfully. At night with a warm fire burning on the log fire hearth I am forcibly reminded of cabin life in the far west. I now don't wonder how old trappers and Hunters keep themselves from freezing even when pursuing their avocations in the midst of winter. "Truly necessity is the mother of invention."[27]

The rumor of a thirty-day armistice was rife in Washington, where it was embroidered by the fanciful report that General Lee was in the city to negotiate the truce. These yarns must have been the invention of defeatists, for no hint of such a move came from the White House, which did not even bother to refute the rumors.

The arrest of Major Watson's assistant surgeons suggests that McKnight was a difficult and unpredictable man. Elaborating upon this theme in a long letter to his father on December 1, the major described internal troubles besetting himself and the regiment:

Dr. Ewing and Wenger were released from arrest this morning—Genl. Birney having disapproved the charges preferred against them. They were of a very trivial nature. Heretofore I have abstained from saying anything concerning Col. McKnight. I now inform you he is capable of any duplicity and meanness. I have avoided this topic as long as I could consistently with justice and self respect. He don't like me—because I stand in the way of Doct. Heichold's reappointment to the Regt. I see he is determined to have Heichold back. Heichold resigned during the Colonel's absence on account of some difficulty with Genl. Robinson. Some weeks ago he got up a Petition requesting Dr. Heichold's reinstatement. . . . It contains his explanation to me. Subsequent facts have induced me to believe that his explanation was not sincere nor given in good faith. The Regiment is about being consolidated and all the officers friendly to me and who refused to sign the petition, with the exception of the Major and Ewing, will be mustered out. Col. McKnight does not possess one iota of refinement and treats his officers more like dogs than men. He seizes with avidity every opportunity of rendering my connection with the Regt. unpleasant. I am under constant espionage and know he is anxiously seeking for some pretext to Court Martial and disgrace me. It is needless to say he is very unpopular and the officers about being mustered out are much rejoiced at the prospect of getting from under his authority in an honorable way. . . . From what I have stated you will observe that a longer connection with this Regt., to say the least of it, will be very disagreeable. Notwithstanding the Colonel I can remain here as long as I choose but the situation would be decidedly uncomfortable. You will at once see I cannot resign without reflecting dishonor on myself. I must either be transferred to an other army situation or remain where I am. . . . I will not resign or leave the Regt. without positive assurance that I shall secure an other appointment—as it would be extremely dis-

graceful to resign when in face of the enemy. Dr. Ewing, 1st Assistant Surgeon, is a Gentleman and a warm and particular personal friend of mine. He says if I leave he will not remain in the Regiment if he can honorably get away. I have the great satisfaction of knowing that no fault has been found with the medical department of this Regt. since under my charge. It is admitted by all to have been conducted as well as any department could be under the circumstances. Still this will make no difference with the Colonel—who is capable of using any means, no matter how foul, in removing and disgracing an officer obnoxious to himself. . . . I like the Medical Officers of this Brigade very well. They are mostly young men. The "Dogs of war" may be let loose at any moment. Two great and hostile armies are lying within striking distance ready and eager for the fray. I only hope a battle will soon ensue—as I should like to be present when the great and decisive engagement of the war is fought. . . . The Paymaster has not come yet—and I saw in yesterday's paper the Paymaster General has made a request for sixty millions more than the treasury contains. If this be so we will not receive our pay until the 1st January. This letter I will mail in an other Regt. Col. McKnight's Postmaster might not scruple to tamper with the letters. . . . Now don't imagine that I am unhappily situated—for I get along better now than at first. But I merely wish to be prepared for the change about to occur in the Regt. You know I possess a certain amount of independence— and you may rest assured I won't tamely submit to any indignity even from a Colonel. My rank entitles me to a certain amount of respect—and you may be sure I demand it.[28]

The major's transfer to another regiment was unnecessary, as the colonel's machinations collapsed when he learned that a new regulation debarred from reappointment a surgeon who had once resigned. The maneuvering Dr. Heichold was permanently out, and Major Watson remained with the 105th Pennsylvania to the end of the war.

Having blown off steam, he was soon his exuberant self again, describing for his sister Emma "the best hospital Quarters in the whole Brigade"—a big new tent and a solid log house with fireplace, built by army pioneers—and again reflecting, though more amiably this time, on the perplexing character of his regimental commander. "I can now visit with pleasure my Hospital," he wrote on December 2:

> *Before it was really distressing to see the poor sick fellows lying on the ground sheltered from the cold and inclement weather by only one old tattered fly. I have been sadly in need of medicine the past few weeks. Tomorrow I will receive a fresh supply. One other source of congratulation is the riddance by discharge of a great many of my old chronic cases. They were constant inmates of the Hospital or regular attendants at the sick call every morning. Last but not least is the positive certainty that we will make a speedy advance. This may occur inside of twenty four hours. Many Gun Boats are on the Rappahannock for the purpose of protecting our crossing the river. The Pontoons are all ready down the river near King George's Court House for erection. A big fight will doubtless ensue. . . . The Phila. Enquirer of today states that twenty thousand men are required to fill up the Pa. Regts. It further states the 105th requires six hundred to fill it up. It think it impossible to get this number. The probability therefore is that old Regts. will be consolidated with old. This may muster me out of the service—as the Com-*

mission of the Surgeon attached to the Regt. consolidated with ours may date prior to mine. In this event I only hope the consolidation will not occur until the finale of this campaign. I have gone through the roughest part of it—and therefore desire to see it through. When we remain long in one place in Camp I always get the "blues." I then generally have but little to do—though I can't complain on this account for the past few days. Just think of it—in a Regt. containing but 280 men there are 3 Surgeons and a Hospital Steward who is a Doctor. One Surgeon could easily do all the business and have plenty of leisure time in the bargain. Many would say this is nothing to complain of—as your pay is the same whether you have much or little to do. On reflection you will see that with nothing to do and nothing to read the Blue devils are necessarily engendered. Our Colonel is rather a disagreeable man when encamped long in one locality. He is a dyspeptic and gets as cross as forty when not actively employed. Has been on a grand rampage for the past few days. But happily for every one under his authority his spleen has subsided and things are progressing more comfortably. He is a very peculiar character—his acts sometimes inducing you to suppose him a very fair and indulgent commander. But a violent exhibition of temper and tyranny suddenly advises you that it has been merely the calm before the storm. He treats me as fairly, however, as any of his Officers. How well that is "deponent saith not."[29]

TWO DAYS LATER, on December 4, Major Watson took time to pen an affectionate, teasing, mildly satirical letter to his youngest sister, twelve-year-old Marie, called "Puddie." He was also newsy and pointed, as usual, and since those pontoons were still waiting to be strung across the Rappahannock, he was inclined to revise his previous expectation of a great Union triumph.

> *I trust you will soon find time to reply, although I know you are constantly occupied with your severe studies and extensive correspondence. Still I opine if you try right hard you will find sufficient unemployed time to answer my letter promptly. It will doubtless surprise you to learn that even here in the "Sunny South" Jack frost exhibits his grisly chin every morning and as I "rise with the lark" I have the extreme felicity of seeing him in the zenith of his frosty magnificence. By means of a bright fire I generally succeed in making him beat a hasty retreat. Complimenting him thus I leave him, as I do every other unpleasant visitor, to the tender care of the gods. Southern ladies do not, I find, possess the great refinement and many accomplishments usually attributed [to] them or if possessing do not display them. They excel in nothing but vile and wholesale abuse of the Yankee Nation—which of all nations, as my friend Mary Barclay's song goes, is the "greatest and the best." You, my dear little Pud, would never make a good Secesh. Firstly because you have too little tongue—and secondly you are too modest and demure. I could trust you in Secessia for years without fear of your turning rebel. When you write I wish you to tell me how your big Sisters treat you. I fear they do not indulge you enough. . . . The Girls wish to know whether I desire any woolen stockings. Tell them no. They by this time should be fully aware [that] these articles are never used by their "delicate brother." The box, however, they speak of sending is a bird of quite an other feather. This will be most thankfully received—and no exceptions taken no matter how often repeated. I would only*

suggest that any thing having the least tendency to spoil be well cooked prior to shipping. I would also ask that the express to Washington be paid, for if I should be as poor as at present I will have a good time getting the box. I would like to have a good and neat pair of nice warm gloves. These, if folded in newspaper form, could be sent by mail. . . . Sleeping on the ground is not so uncomfortable as a delicate young lady like you might imagine. Of course it sometimes gets a little colder than when in a warm house covered with huge piles of comforts and blankets. . . . Yesterday was a very pleasant day, being bright and clear. Genl. Birney inspected our Regiment. It is needless to state that your brother in his well worn, rudely patched and only Uniform did not present a very grand or imposing appearance. But a soldier on duty in the field is not expected to be as trim and neat as when rusticating far from the seat of war. Early this morning it began raining—but for the last hour or two it has been snowing. The ground is entirely covered and from present indications I should say we are going to have a long wet spell. This possibly may retard our advance—but in my opinion it will only hasten it, as it is customary for our Generals to remain in Camp during pleasant weather—and do all their hard marching and fighting when mud and rain are in the ascendency. This at least has been my experience since in the service. Concerning our future movements I am in the dark as much as my little Pud. Our Army here consists of three Grand Divisions commanded respectively by Hooker, Sumner and Franklin. Our Corps is in Hooker's grand division. These three divisions number about one hundred thousand troops. The enemy's force is estimated at one hundred and thirty thousand. If this estimate is correct we will not be able to cross the river—

*and even if we were by the aid of the Gun Boats we would in all
probability get soundly whipped after we went over. From [all]
I can hear this campaign has been a failure—in consequence of
Genl. Burnside not receiving the Pontoons as soon as he desired.
. . . How would you like living on hard crackers—so hard that
they must have been made during the war of 1812—salt junk,
Coffee and sugar? These are my rations. The Sutlers bring us
nothing—either because we have no money or because they have
expended all theirs—and are therefore unable to lay in a new
stock. I have not tasted bread and butter for so long that they
would be the greatest luxury I could have. You will remember
how you and I used to turn up our noses at the idea of sitting
down to plain bread and butter. I would enjoy nothing more
now than one of our old wash day dinners.[30]*

The major's one patched uniform and his poverty-stricken
condition reflect the vagaries of an inefficient Union supply system in 1862. He had still received no pay, after
almost three months.

Putting enemy strength at 130,000 was one of those
exaggerations common on the Federal side. In the Peninsula campaign, McClellan had been made overcautious
by the reports of Alan Pinkerton, organizer of the Secret
Service, who estimated Confederate numbers at about
twice the actuality. Before Fredericksburg, Burnside had
six army corps; opposed to them were two corps of the
Army of Northern Virginia, Stuart's cavalry, and an artillery reserve: all told, probably about half the Union
strength. But, granted time to dig in during several weeks
while the two armies merely looked at each other across
the river, the Confederates had the advantage of a strong,

almost impregnable, defensive position, as Burnside was to learn at terrible cost. His officers counseled against crossing the Rappahannock to attack, but the commander, believing that the enemy had weakened his center, ordered the advance. On December 10, the 105th Pennsylvania prepared to move. "I was ordered this morning," wrote Major Watson,

> to send all my sick in hospital to Genl. Hospital and to report for duty every man on the sick list able to march 10 miles or do one day's duty. This would indicate that we are not going to march more than ten miles. But where we are going and for what object is a mystery to me. We are all packed up—and will leave this place tonight. Here my information ceases. The prevailing opinion is that we will embark at Belle Plain for the Peninsula. This place is but 10 miles from us. Many, on the other hand, contend we will cross the Rappahannock and attack the enemy. If we cross tonight we shall in all probability have a fight tomorrow. . . . If we intended merely to change Camp we would transport the sick with us. Dr. Church, Surg. 141 Pa. Vols., sent 169 to Genl. Hospital, the other Regts. in the same proportion. I sent but 29. I had a great time regaining them to day. Many of them wished to remain behind, not caring to engage in [a] fight. Those I found playing off I of course reported for duty. They cursed me right soundly, I understand, after getting out of hearing. This is nothing—for Quinine as the Boys generally call the Surgeon—"Old Quin" gets many a deep though not loud cursing—especially from the lazy vagabonds who try their very best to play sick and so get off duty. Dr. Ewing received a letter from Doct. Heichold to day—informing him that a petition had been sent to the Governor requesting

his reinstatement to the Regt. He seemed very sanguine of success and talked what he would do when he came back. Poor fellow, he will be sadly disappointed. He is a great Republican and has considerable political influence at home, hence he was sure of being reappointed. . . . I am very anxious for an onward move. My horse is no better. I will have him led—though it will be slow work as he can scarcely put his foot to the ground. Our Post Master has lent me his horse—so I will not have to foot it.[31]

AFTER FURTHER DELAY, Union engineers, under hot fire from enemy sharpshooters, completed a pontoon bridge across the river. By the morning of December 13 Burnside's army was on the Fredericksburg side, the troops making a fine show of dress parade spit-and-polish that excited the admiration of Confederate gunners. Then followed, during a long day, six costly assaults upon Marye's Heights, every one sent reeling back. These disastrous attacks exhausted and shattered the Union army, which suffered losses of over 12,000 killed, wounded, and missing. Major Watson was too busy for letters, but on December 15, when the intensity of conflict had subsided, he scribbled a hasty note:

I am very busily engaged—having been employed for four days in attending our wounded. We have had a severe battle or rather series of battles. You will see in the Newspapers a better and more definite account than I would be able to give you even if I had time. I only write this note to let you know that I am well and uninjured. Day before yesterday (Saturday) I was under the fire of shells for several hours. I was standing but a few yards from where Genl. Bayard was shot. Our Division Hospi-

tal is now established on the other side of the river (North side).
I am on the South side today—having been detailed to attend
those who require attention before reaching Division Hospital.
. . . We have not gained much from the enemy. Still all are sanguine of success. We only lost in our Regt., as far as I can ascertain, 6 wounded and 2 killed. Capt. Hamilton, my particular
friend and by far the finest Officer in the Regt., had his right
arm very badly torn by a shell. When they explode near one they
make a very ugly noise. I only trust I shall never witness another battle. I have had enough Surgery now to do me for quite
a number of years. Tomorrow, I think, will be the great and
decisive battle of Battles. I only trust we will be victorious. Our
Division lost in killed and wounded between eight hundred and
a thousand. . . . Our Brigade behaved splendidly. The Zouaves
and 68 Pa. were principally engaged—the rest of the Regts. being held to support the batteries. Genl. Robinson had a horse
shot from under him. . . . Our troops, who had always disliked
Genl. Robinson, saying he did not like the smell of powder, now
say he is as brave as a lion and cheer him every time he passes
the lines. Genl. Birney handled his Division admirably. In fact
both Officers and troops behaved most gallantly. There was no
straggling. . . . I extracted balls and dressed the wounds of about
twenty Secesh. They belonged to Genl. Jackson's Corps. He commands the enemy's right and as we are cooperating with
Franklin, who commands our left, we have been opposed to
him. And when troops, knowing who they are fighting against,
fight as well as ours—victory is almost sure to follow. [A half
page here is too blurry and faded to be legible.] You must excuse
this letter. If you read it you can do more than I can—but it is
written in the greatest possible haste.[32]

Major Watson's comment that newspapers would give a better summary of the battle than he could is a reminder that in the turmoil of action the soldier knew only what happened in his immediate vicinity.

Wholesome respect for Jackson was universal in the Union army. Major Watson's praise of troops pitted against this formidable tactician celebrates one of those moral victories gained by the loser. But the major's hopes of success in the field were not fulfilled. After six repulses, Burnside planned still another assault, but this time he was overruled. On December 15 the broken Union army began withdrawing to the north bank of the Rappahannock, where it went into winter quarters near Falmouth, Virginia, to nurse its wounds. Burnside assumed responsibility for the failure of the Fredericksburg offensive, but no explanation stayed the noisy clamor of home front editors and patriots enraged by another Union reverse.

MAJOR WATSON, having been temporarily detailed to general hospital duty, rejoined his regiment on December 21. "I am very well satisfied to get back to the Regt.," he wrote that day to his sister Ella,

> as I was heartily sick of witnessing the suffering of our brave soldiers. The weather has been extremely cold the past few days— and particularly so today. The Hospital tents are not provided with Stoves. Consequently the wounded suffered much—some of them nearly freezing. We were fortunate in having warm and pleasant weather during the fight—as the troops forming our advanced lines were compelled to lie closely to the ground

without fires from Saturday morning till Monday night. Had the weather been as severe as now the men could not possibly have stood it. Being in an open plain immediately in front of the enemy's position they dare not make even a cup of Coffee—lest Grape and Shell be hailed at them. New Regts. are continually arriving. . . . Some of these new Regts. have no tents. God knows how they endure the cold without perishing. I have no stove and sleep on the ground covered by rather an indifferent old tent. Still live vastly more comfortable than they. I have a horse and can carry plenty of good warm blankets while the poor soldier with his gun, cartridge box and heavy knapsack finds it impossible to carry more than one or two blankets. Yet in the face of all this "Winter Quarters" are loudly denounced and "Onward to Richmond" importunately demanded by lazy Editors and idle Senators and Congressmen living at home in shameless and inglorious ease. I would like to have them here during this inclement weather—compel them to shoulder a musket—with Cartridge box containing eight pounds of Cartridges. Carry a heavy Knapsack and lie shivering through the entire night on the cold and damp ground, and my word for it—these stay at home warlike gentlemen will soon change their tune. I don't want the Army to go into winter quarters—because a vigorous and energetic prosecution of the war is demanded to quash the rebellion. But don't keep the Army a whole month freezing in sight of a hostile city—giving the enemy full and ample time to render his position impregnable. This is the history of the famous campaign of the Rappahannock. A policy of this kind will demoralize the best disciplined and most patriotic Army in the world. If the President desires success he must permit the Generals in the field to conduct the campaign—not

*Genl. Halleck and Mr. Stanton. What will be done in the future
I am not even able to conjecture. But I hope, pray and trust it
may not be attended with defeat. . . . The Pay Master has not
arrived yet—and as he has been so long about it I only hope he
won't come till after 1st January. Should he come before, I will
only get a month and a half's pay. If he don't come till 1st
January I will be mustered for pay to this date—hence will
receive 3 months and half pay. This will make a considerable
difference—so I could cheerfully wait a week or two longer. I
informed Pa in my letter how to direct my box. I only hope I
will receive it—as I am heartily sick of Army rations. I would
give a great deal to spend the Holidays with you. But it cannot
be. So I will comfort myself thinking what a good time I would
have if there.*[33]

A̶S WE LOOK BACK at the Fredericksburg debacle, the
frontal attack upon an enemy given ample time to fortify himself seems to have been ill-advised. Interference
from Washington plagued all Union armies, partly because government authorities took heed of political implications as well as military ones. Major General Henry W.
Halleck, acting as a sort of chief of staff in the capital,
attempted to run the war by remote control. Known as
"Old Brains," he had the reputation of being an excellent book soldier, but he was so cautious and slow, so far
from the scene of action, that he could be a hindrance to
energetic commanders in the field. Secretary of War
Edwin Stanton and even Lincoln took a hand at directing army movements. But sometimes their views were
more sensible than those of generals. Burnside, in his

report on the Fredericksburg campaign, admitted that Lincoln, Halleck, and Stanton had all opposed the operation but had finally given the commander leave to proceed as he wished. Events this time proved the armchair strategists right, the general wrong.

As 1862 ended, Union hopes in the eastern theater of war floundered in a morass of ineptitude. Burnside, although a competent Corps commander, had been no more successful as leader of the Army of the Potomac than his predecessors, McClellan and Pope. On December 28, Major Watson, who did not receive the promised box from home (it never did reach him), reported spending a miserable Christmas. Then, like many another soldier, he took off on an exposition of how the war should be fought, and reminisced about his experiences during the Battle of Fredericksburg:

> *I have been very busy ever since the battle and will continue to be so for the next week or two. I have a monthly and Quarterly report to make out this week, also the annual return of Hospital property and supplies. The return embraces a correct report of all supplies received and expended during the year—also what remains on hand. . . . I spent a very dull and dry old Christmas. My bill of fare for Dinner consisted of "Hard tack," Corned Beef, Beans and Coffee. If the box don't come by New Year's I will have a repetition of my Christmas Dinner. You take a gloomy view, my dear Pa, of our future success. The Army is not demoralized in the least—and is as willing to be led against the enemy now as before crossing the Rappahannock. I should dislike to again witness the death and suffering of so many of our brave boys without more being gained. Yet I am satisfied if we*

have sufficient force we can whip the rebels even behind their intrenchments. Had we had double our present force we could have defeated them in the recent battle. The Government has the troops and why were they not sent here instead of to other less important points? I say give the Army of the Potomac ten to one against the rebels and let us defeat and disorganize their Army in Virginia and the Rebellion will soon cease to exist. What is the use of making distant and expensive expeditions against unimportant points? Concentrate our forces and drive the enemy out of their strongholds in Virginia and the war must cease. It is true that our repulse has created some little dissatisfaction in the Army. But not with Burnside. Let Burnside continue in command and McClellan take Halleck's place and almost the whole Army will rejoice. During the fight there were thousands upon thousands of shell thrown. One soon gets accustomed to them although they make a most frightful and terrific noise. The morning after recrossing the river our Division Hospital was again removed. It was established first on the South side— then moved to a woods on the North side. When the Army retreated I was on duty on the South side—had charge of a kind of branch Division Hospital on that side. I came over with the Army and reported at Division Hospital. I was immediately detailed to superintend loading the Ambulances—as the Hospital was to be moved some 3 miles to the rear. The Shell came into the woods pretty thick—and all the Surgeons not on duty got out as soon as possible. I must confess I felt a little nervous at first. But knowing it was my duty to remain until all the wounded were removed—I paid no further attention to them. They did not come any thing like as near and thick as on Saturday. That was shelling. Generally Division Hospital is not within shot or shell range. But on this occasion necessity compelled us to establish it on the South side—and as the enemy were only a mile or so of the river we were within easy range the entire time. I was under fire from Saturday morning till Monday night. I have had surgery enough to do me a great while. . . . We have not been paid yet but in all human probability will be in a few weeks—when if I have an opportunity I will be able to send you between four and five hundred dollars. There is no express office nearer than Washington and there may be some difficulty in getting the money there. You may rest assured I will retain it about me as short a time as possible. The Army contains a great many thieves. I have not forgotten the loss of my overcoat yet. I have not one cent of money—nor one postage stamp. The latter cannot be gotten for either love or money. I will try and borrow one—and if I fail will have to get this letter franked. Don't like to do it—"But necessity knows no law." . . . My horse is completely recovered. He stood fire well. I was on him right under a hill on which was a large siege gun. When discharged it shook the very earth—but he never paid the least attention to it.[34]

Apropos of the major's remark about giving the Army of the Potomac "ten to one against the rebels," it generally outnumbered the enemy in battle, but this advantage was more than offset by bold Confederate leadership. Union armies needed troops less than assured commanders capable of matching wits with Lee, Jackson, Longstreet, Stuart, and their able associates. So far no such Union general had appeared. The belief that the Virginia theater of war was the only important one was commonly held in the East. Yet tightening the naval blockade, capture of southern Atlantic ports, opening the Mississippi River, and campaigns in Kentucky and Missouri were also important. Exploits like the taking of Forts Henry and Donelson, in Tennessee, by an obscure officer named Ulysses Grant in February 1862 were to lead to momentous events.

The major, ending the year without a cent or even a postage stamp, is a sad commentary on a woefully inadequate supply system. That department of this army, like its generalship in the field, needed time to become efficient.

1863

*T*HE ARRIVAL OF A NEW YEAR brought no immediate change in the major's hand-to-mouth living. Yet, inclined to make the best of things and buoyed by the hope of receiving that box from home, he seldom seemed low-spirited. "Your last letter," he wrote his sister Ella on January 4, 1863,

> *contained five dollars and the Express receipt. I don't think there is any danger of the box not reaching me safely provided it was well secured. . . . I have been to Aquia Creek twice the past week. Was there yesterday. There are tons upon tons of Express matter for our Grand Division. But every thing passes through the hands of the Provost. I enquired when he would have the boxes shipped to Falmouth. He replied there were so d——d many that he did not know if he would ever get them all up. . . . Yesterday I went down for the purpose of procuring some things from the Sanitary Commission and I give you my word I had not money enough nor could I borrow it to get my dinner. And furthermore if it were not for "old Pap," my cook, I would be compelled to beg my rations or starve. Old Pap has a little money*

which he kindly permits me to make use of—or rather he expends it for me in the purchase of Crackers, Coffee and Sugar. So you can imagine how delighted I was to receive even five dollars. Dr. Wenger started immediately with it to buy some smoking tobacco, a luxury we have been unable to enjoy for some time. He returned saying the Sutler refused taking it, saying it was not good money. But I will try again before sending it back. I would be obliged to Pa if he would send me some Postage stamps. . . . Dr. Jones, our Med. Direct., has applied for leave of absence. The Genl. commanding the Brigade (we have a new Genl., Genl. Robinson having been put in Command of Gibbon's Division) said if he could get a competent person to fill his place he would approve the application. The Doct. came and requested me to act. I thanked him and told him I would do so with pleasure. . . . The Doct. also said if we had an other battle I would be appointed Chief Operator for the Brigade. So you see I am getting along first rate. Dr. Ewing, 1st Asst., a very nice fellow by the way, is very tired of the service. Says he wishes to see his wife and children and will tender his resignation tomorrow. Dr. Wenger, my other Assist., is very sick of playing soldier. The service would lose nothing in losing him. He knows nothing. Consequently is of no use to me. . . . Col. McKnight has been very sick—had Erysipelas—but is now convalescing. He seems to think I am a great Doctor and makes a great deal of me now. I have talked so much about myself in this and a former letter that you will think my bump of self esteem is greatly increasing. I will not deny that this organ is pretty largely developed. But as I informed you some time ago that I was not getting along very pleasantly I thought it my duty to let you know "that times is changed" and I am doing splendidly. . . . In my opinion we will soon have hard work to do. I for one desire

*a speedy advance. We are stronger now than we will be in a
month or six months. The Army is being decimated by sickness
every day. We have sufficient force, if handled properly, to whip
the rebs to death. I trust Genl. Rosecrans will gain a complete
victory in Tennessee.*[1]

Major General William S. Rosecrans, having assumed
command of the Army of the Cumberland in the fall of
1862, had marched to Nashville, where he spent a month
outfitting his troops. Then he took off southward to engage the Confederate army of General Braxton Bragg.
The dogged three-days' battle at Murfreesboro, or Stones
River, December 31–January 2, was more indecisive than
otherwise, but it has been called a Union victory, mainly
because Bragg withdrew after the third day.

For the Army of the Potomac, action was, as the
major surmised, imminent. Burnside's new plan, unani-
mously approved by his staff, was to cross the Rappahannock above Falmouth and, in a surprise thrust, flank
the defenders of Fredericksburg and take them in the
rear. On January 15, Major Watson once again received
marching orders. "I am very busily engaged," he wrote
his father on that day,

> *sending sick to Division Hospital. We will move tomorrow, prob-
> ably to night. I think we will cross the river. Genl. Sumner's
> Division received orders last night. Pontoons were immediately
> sent to the river. By the time you receive this doubtless you will
> have heard of an other great battle on the Rappahannock. I
> trust we shall meet with better success. . . . I have not seen or
> heard any thing of the Box—and as we move will probably
> never see it. Should it turn up in future every thing will be*

*spoiled. . . . The Paymaster has not arrived—and I fear will not
for some time. I am entirely out of money—and if you can spare
any will be much obliged for a little—just enough to buy cigars
and an occasional lump of butter. . . . The Government is in-
debted to me over six hundred dollars and here I am ragged,
dirty, and to tell the truth slightly lousy. I do say Uncle Sam
treats his Officers more like Dogs than Gentlemen. If the Government would permit the Express Company to make use of the
railroad—we would have our boxes. Now there are thousands
upon thousands at Aquia and Belle Plain and no way of getting them up. But they are only for the soldiers and the poor
soldier is nobody. . . . I have passed through one hard campaign—witnessed one bloody battle and had as much surgery
as I desired. So I did not care about engaging in an other drama
like this. But it must be so. Therefore I trust I may escape as
well in this as the former.*[2]

Those thousands of undelivered Christmas boxes imply
an official obtuseness that seemed unaware of the mo-
rale-building effect of homemade pies and cookies upon
the spirits of lonely soldiers. A few army wagons manned
by husky squads could have brought these gifts into
camp, but evidently nobody thought of that.

As usual, the imminence of speedy movement
turned out to be less imminent than expected. Two days
later, the army was still immobile. Meanwhile, bringing
up pontoons by back roads and a general stir of preparation in the Union camp had alerted Confederate spies
and pickets, thus dimming the hope of taking the enemy
by surprise. "We are still here," wrote Major Watson to
his sister Ella on January 17:

Had a hard rain with a tremendous gale—but were to move this morning at 6 o'clock. This was countermanded last night by an order stating we would leave Sunday [January 18] at 1 o'clock. I can't account for this delay—unless the weather was deemed too cold for the men to lie out—or the wind may have interfered with the construction of the Pontoon bridges. . . . I fear many a poor fellow unable to carry more than one blanket will freeze to death—for it is bitter cold. The Medical department has received the usual orders preparatory to a battle. So there is no doubt that many a good soldier will again fall in defence of his country. I only trust the blood of our brave soldiers will not be expended in vain. It is pretty hard for us to leave our comfortable quarters during this cold weather. Many of the men have gone to the trouble and labor of building log Houses. Still there are no complaints—and every man is ready and willing to do his duty. Truly the American soldier demands the admiration of the whole world. He is ever cheerful, courageous and non complaining. Defeated to day, he willingly and cheerfully renews the conflict tomorrow. These characteristics must and will end in glorious success. . . . The box, I fear, is lost. Have never heard of it—although I have sent frequently to the Express Depots. I am very sorry—as I had promised myself a rare feast on your good things. You will please thank for me all contributors. Col. McKnight is trying to have our Regt. consolidated [with] the 57th and 99th Pa. Regts. The whole three will make but one full Regt. He desires the command. . . . If an arrangement of this kind is made only one Surgeon will be retained. Being old Regts. the Commissions of both Surgeons, I presume, date prior to mine. This entitles them to the first say— to stay or quit the service just as they please. Should they both

desire to leave then I will have to remain. If, on the other hand,
one of them wishes to remain then I will have to go. So you see
I have no option in the matter at all. The fact is I don't care
what they do. I shall be perfectly satisfied either way.[3]

The major's glowing portrait of the soldier as always cheerful and uncomplaining seems unduly romantic. The Civil
War veteran, like his American counterpart before and
since, was a swearing, grousing, hard-bitten fellow less
concerned with patriotic ideals than with the mundane
business of eating, sleeping, and dodging enemy bullets.
But he was, as the major implied, a good fighting man
who needed only skillful leadership to make his prowess
count. That his bravery would have a fair chance to strike
a positive blow on this campaign was problematical.

The army did not move, the weather worsened, and
the enemy by this time were well aware of Burnside's
intentions. On January 19, the major wrote:

We were to leave on Saturday but the order was countermanded
for 24 hours. Since then this order has been daily counter-
manded. We are packed up and ready to leave at a moment's
notice. The time fixed is 1 o'clock tomorrow. So if not otherwise
ordered tomorrow we go. I understand Genl. Franklin's Divi-
sion will remain—only Hooker and Sumner go. No person here
has the slightest knowledge of our intended route. A flank move-
ment cannot be contemplated—as every person in the Army
has known for the past week that we were going to march. This
intelligence, of course, has already been conveyed to the enemy—
who will of course be fully prepared for us. The campaign (if
there be one contemplated) is enveloped in mystery—no one
knowing any thing about it except those high in authority—

and I only trust our plans are equally obscure to the enemy. . . . Yesterday the whole Brigade was ordered out under arms to witness the punishment of a malefactor—the offense desertion. The Brigade was formed into two lines about seventy five paces apart facing each other. The culprit was taken to the centre, his head shaved, the letter D branded on his hip—his buttons cut off and then marched hat in hand in advance of a file of eight men with charged bayonets the entire extent of both lines—the Band following in the rear playing the Rogue's March. In this way he was conducted [a] half mile beyond the limits of the Camp. He doubtless deserved the punishment—although it was cruelly severe. Not a cheer was given, solemnity and sympathy being imprinted on every countenance. The effect will be beneficial—as many have threatened desertion as soon as paid off. Speaking of pay reminds me that the Paymaster is still "non est." When he comes I fear he will only pay to the 1st Nov. This will leave me due from the Government about five hundred dollars. . . . I am obliged to keep a supervisory eye over Wenger. He has sometimes reported men fit for duty who were too sick to carry a gun—letting others capable of doing duty off—they telling him a very piteous and distressing story of their sufferings. Now if I tell him this he will put sick men on duty to avoid being imposed on. You will readily see that his professional abilities are limited. He is not a graduate and should not have been commissioned. . . . The box has not arrived. Fear I shall lose it.[4]

AT LAST THE ARMY MOVED. The commands of Generals Joseph Hooker and William Franklin marched on January 20 toward Banks' Ford, above Falmouth, about ten miles from camp. Heavy rains had turned roads into a mass of sticky clay through which infantry floundered. Four and six horses hitched to a pontoon, 150 men tugging on long ropes attached to one of those cumbersome boats, could not get up enough pontoons to bridge the river. Artillery became hopelessly mired. Part of Franklin's troops, having taken the wrong road, tried to cut across the center, and in the dark, the rain, and the mud, created chaotic confusion.

By January 22 Burnside's disordered troops, strung out for several miles on a route littered with abandoned pontoons, overturned wagons, dead mules, and stragglers looking for their regiments, looked like an army that had gone through a hard battle. Haversack rations were about to give out, and supply trains were stuck far in the rear. All chance of surprise was gone; at Banks' Ford Confederate pickets on the other side jeeringly asked the Yanks if they needed help. There was nothing to do but plod back to camp. Thus ended an abortive campaign that came to be known as Burnside's "Mud March." Reporting this fiasco on January 27, Major Watson seemed reasonably cheerful:

> *Last Tuesday our whole Army, with the exception of Genl. Sumner's Corps, moved some eight miles up the river for the purpose of crossing and attacking the Enemy. But unfortunately it rained—rendering the roads so muddy that the Pontoons and Batteries could not be brought up. Recently the rebel force has been much diminished—while ours has been greatly increased—and had the good weather continued I am satisfied we could have crossed over and completely routed them with half the loss sustained in the former battle. The men were all*

eager for fight and sanguine of success. But the Pontoons sticking fast in the mud rendered the construction of the Bridges impossible. So we were ordered to return to our old camp. This order was received in stern silence—every face expressing chagrin and disappointment. Soldiers always dislike to fall back especially when sure of victory. All reports stating the Army of the Potomac is demoralized and unwilling to again face the enemy are false. The troops were never in finer spirits and more desirous of engaging the rebels. But I fear we will have a long period of inactivity—as a winter campaign in this latitude of mud and rain is impracticable. . . . I have applied for 3 days' leave of absence to visit Washington for the purpose of procuring Clothing and other necessaries. Hope I will get it. Had not my 1st Asst. Surgeon been detailed for Hospital duty I think I could have had a leave of 10 or 20 days. . . . Should like very much to pay a short visit home.[5]

The Army of the Potomac, if not demoralized, was yet depressed by frequent promises of successful offensives that had too often fizzled out in rebuffs followed by retreat. The recent mud campaign was evidently one frustration too many for General Burnside, who was relieved after about ten weeks as commander of this army. On January 26, a new commander took over, Major General Hooker.

Major Watson did not get his three days' leave. But having at long last been paid after four payless months—a miracle he somehow failed to mention—he entrusted money and instructions for buying clothes to another doctor headed for Washington. "I sent sixty five dollars for this purpose," he wrote on January 30:

Therefore hope to be both decently and comfortably clad. I have worn a thin flannel suit all winter and strange to say, notwithstanding all my exposure, have never enjoyed better health. Have not had one twinge of my old enemy, the Rheumatism. I also ·sent with him one hundred and twenty five dollars which he will express in Phila. to Pa. I would like to have sent more— but could not as I only received one month and 14 days pay. I understand that owing to the scarcity of wood we will be compelled to move Camp. All the woods near us have been cut down and consumed. . . . Genl. Hooker is now commander of the Army of the Potomac. I am sorry for this—although he is an able and gallant Officer. The Army loses with great reluctance the gallant and magnanimous Burnside. True, his efforts were unattended with success and his plans have resulted in failure. But this was owing to a combination of unfortunate circumstances over which he had no control. His last effort, promising such brilliant results, was defeated by Divine, not by human agencies. . . . If the administration deemed him incapable of Commanding—why did they not return to the Army its pet and ideal, Genl. McClellan? This, like all other well disciplined armies, will fight well under the leadership of any General. Still an unprejudiced person will admit that the presence of McClellan would have instilled new ardor and irresistible courage. The soldiers will fight bravely under the gallant Hooker. But under McClellan joyfully and enthusiastically. In my opinion we will not be able to move for six weeks or two months. The roads are almost without bottom.[6]

The comments about commanders are interesting in that they reflect on qualifications that made an officer fit to command. Burnside was, as the major said, gallant and magnanimous. He was a capable Corps commander, but handling an army was too much for him. McClellan undoubtedly could have inspired troops to fight hard, yet his reluctance to fight had been the very shortcoming that had caused his removal. A good officer in one echelon was not necessarily good if advanced to a more responsible post. Leaders on both sides discovered that an efficient brigadier, who carried out orders with vigor and dispatch, might cave in under the burden of corps command; an effective general of a division might be entirely at sea as commander of an army. The soldier in the field was aware of these variables only dimly, if at all, but Lincoln knew of them, and so did Lee.

Lincoln had reservations about Hooker, having cautioned him to "Beware of rashness" yet hoping that he might bring victory to Union arms. The new commander made a spectacular show on his white horse, and he had a profane swagger that gave point to his sobriquet of "Fighting Joe." But as the major surmised, the Army of the Potomac was immobilized for more than two months by wet weather and soggy terrain. Faced again with the monotony of camp life, Major Watson relayed to his family such items as came to hand. In a long letter to his father on February 2, he discussed the provocative question of enlisting black troops:

> I am sorry, though not surprised, to learn that the democrats
> are bent on defeating any and every measure of the administra-
> tion. I am far from endorsing "in toto" Mr. Lincoln's policy. He
> is too much swayed by the radicals to suit me—and they seem
> determined to outrage beyond endurance the feelings of the

Northern conservatists and Border State Unionists by forcing through Congress the bill for the organization of Negro Regts. I am entirely and unconditionally opposed to this bill. And I am certain I am speaking the true sentiment of the Army of the Potomac when I say not one Officer in twenty can be found willing to accept command in these Regts. . . . . At best it is but an experiment—for in the first place we don't know whether the Negro will enlist—and secondly are not sure they will fight even when enlisted. Instead of this nigger question, if the administration with Congress will devote itself entirely to our financial affairs and the vigorous prosecution of the war the rebellion will be suppressed in less time than it will take to organize, equip and discipline the niggers. Place a black Regt. side by side with the 105th and this Regt., though composed almost entirely of Republicans, would charge and drive them with more delight than they would the rebels. I don't say I approve of this—but I do say it would be done. In my opinion the passage of this bill will tend to the demoralization of our Army and to the success of the rebels. You have no idea how greatly the common soldiers are prejudiced against the Negro. An officer can scarcely retain a colored servant. I have seen with pity and indignation [a] poor, unfortunate and inoffensive contraband kicked, cuffed and maltreated without cause. The soldiers do this because they think the Negro considers himself their equal and that before long he will be made so by Congress and the administration. Therefore I say it is impolitic to agitate this question more at present. But it seems the Radicals would sooner let the Union "slide" than slavery continue—while the butternut Democrats would sooner let the Union than slavery slide. There is no difference between them—for neither desire the reconstruction of the Union as it was. If the North remain united the rebels must succumb. But I fear we shall be defeated by political dissension. Lieut. Nesbit, a friend of mine, received a letter from his Sister living in Washington. She is a great republican. Says that Stanton is universally execrated by all parties—and that "poor old Abe is snubbed by every one except Stanton." That Stanton is thought to have entrapped the President into some dirty speculating tricks and now holds the whip hand over him. She says Stanton controls, through the President, the Cabinet. I think this more than likely. And I fear the President deserves no longer the "Soubriquet" of "Honest old Abe." . . . The roads are impassable even for Provision trains. How then can Ammunition trains and heavy Artillery be got along? At present it will require at least 12 or 14 horses to pull a single six pounder. The New York Herald demands that Genl. Hooker shall redeem his promise by advancing as soon as the roads "dry up" or "freeze over." It lauds Hooker to the skies and then remarks that the Army of the Potomac should not be kept in "shameful and demoralizing idleness." I am certain it is endeavoring to push Hooker on for the purpose of having him defeated. . . . The Herald knows perfectly well that the ground will not remain frozen any time in this latitude—and that a thaw will certainly retard an advance as well as prevent a retreat. Such an advance would surely result in an other mud fight. I believe the command of this Army will ruin Hooker as it did McClellan, Pope and Burnside for it has been and I fear always will be controlled by the administration, not by the Genl. commanding. Yesterday the Colonel and I took a ride. . . . we stopped at a signal station for the purpose of taking a "squint" at Rebeldom through a "field glass." The extent and magnitude of the fortifications surprised me. The crests of the hills are dotted with redoubts connected by rifle pits. These redoubts extend for miles on each side of the town. Their lines of defense, four or five in number, commence immediately in the rear of Fredericksburg and extend to the top of the Hills. . . . . I don't think Jackson was idly boasting when he said that with his own Division he could hold the position against our entire Army. It looks impregnable any how. In my opinion we will never get to Richmond if we take this route. Genl. Hooker, however, may think differently and again assault them. Yesterday Doct. Ewing sent for me to visit him at Division Hospital. He is pretty sick. . . . My other Assistant, dutchman like, does nothing but eat and sleep. I am a good—very good feeder as you know. Well, without exaggeration, he consumes four times the quantity I do—always continues his repast long after I have finished and then, anaconda like, remains in a stupor till the next meal, at which time he is always sure to "rouse up." When not thus engaged he is polishing up his soldier's buttons. Has no horse— therefore foots it. Through charity I have carried his blankets on my horse and invited him to bunk with me. I thought he could not afford to buy a horse. So when the Paymaster came I went to him and so presented the case. He was only commissioned in November and hence entitled to no pay. After much persuasion the paymaster paid him to the 1st January. This gave him almost as much pay as myself. Still, although I have repeatedly urged him, he has shown no disposition to purchase a horse. I have only to say that in future he will have to carry his own blankets and sleep by himself. Had I known what I do now I would have had those two months pay for myself. When we get where we will have picket duty to do, I bet I will tire his legs for him. He is no assistance to me. Neither is he companionable. I would most willingly do without him. . . . . The Colo-

nel just informed me that tomorrow there will be a rigid inspection of the Medical Dept. of his Regt. by a board appointed by Birney. My records, prescription Book, Hospital instruments and all cases reported sick will be examined. I am prepared, so let them come—for I flatter myself that my Department will compare with any in the Division.[7]

The strong racial prejudices of the soldiers are not unlike those still with us more than one hundred years later. The belief that black troops might not fight was later disproved, and the reluctance of white officers to command them countered by the meritorious service of such leaders as Colonel Robert Gould Shaw, white commander of the 54th Massachusetts, an all-black regiment. The stories buzzing around Washington about Lincoln and Stanton reveal that the capital was as gossipy then as it is today. People might have believed that Stanton was the power behind the President, yet historians make clear that from the outset Lincoln ruled the Cabinet, as he demonstrated to William Henry Seward, Salmon Chase, Stanton, and any other inclined to contest his control. As civilian commander-in-chief, he also controlled the army, as the major said. The reason was that Lincoln was constantly aware, as generals and soldiers often were not, of political as well as military implications.

Major Watson's belief that General Hooker was headed for failure was uncannily accurate. This commander of the Army of the Potomac lasted just five months. The major weathered the inspection of his department with great success. "The Medical Board has just left," he wrote on February 3, *after a thorough inspection of every thing pertaining to my De-partment. They complimented me highly—saying these inspec-tions would be unnecessary if every Surgeon conducted his department as well. Dr. Lyman remarked, "Why, Doct., you re-port but 24 sick—and ¾ of them have very little the matter with them." I said that is true, Doct., but you know I must have a sick list or every one will forget that I am a Surgeon in the Army. They all laughed very much at this—so we separated mutually pleased with one an other. The weather is extremely cold today—so cold that an overcoat is comfortable sitting in a tent. The roads will bear Artillery today. Therefore I suppose all the non combatants up north will be "crying onward to Rich-mond." Soldiers sleeping without tents in such weather would soon be used up.[8]*

A̶FTER THAT LETTER a long hiatus of more than a month occurs in the major's correspondence. During this time he got an extended leave and spent a few weeks at home. By March 1 he was again in camp. He defied prejudice by bringing with him from Bedford a young African American named Henry, who acted as an orderly of sorts. "Some days ago," the major wrote on March 8,

> *our Brigade moved some five miles from here in the direction of Belle Plain. The scarcity of wood rendered this move necessary. I was too unwell to go with the Regt.—so I came here to Division Hospital. I have now entirely recovered and will rejoin my Regt. tomorrow. One of our Boys came to see me yesterday. Said we had a delightful Camp—plenty of wood and good water. I am glad I returned to the Regt. on time. Some of the Officers, by overstaying their time, have got into trouble. . . . I am very*

much pleased with Henry. He is a very good Boy—and seems to be delighted with his situation.[9]

$\mathcal{A}$NOTHER BREAK OF A MONTH OCCURS in the letters here. On April 6 he wrote his sister Eliza:

The roads were drying up splendidly and we all expected a speedy move. But an unfortunate snow storm has knocked every thing in the head. Why, day before yesterday we had four inches of snow and now the roads are almost as bad as ever. Sunday morning our Regt. went on 3 days' picket. The picket line is about six miles from here. They must have had an awful march for they started just in the midst of the snow storm. Yesterday the President visited the Army. He looks badly. He was present at a grand Cavalry Review accompanied by Genl. Hooker and all the minor military celebrities. There were plenty of Ladies present on horse back. I have been appointed Operator in Chief of the Brigade. . . . These appointments are made according to merit, regardless of rank. You now know there is at least one distinguished and meritorious individual in the Watson family. . . . I had intended saying a good deal about my Sisters not writing me oftener but I believe I won't. I will just mention it. Conscience will do the rest. There is no indication at present of a move. The Pay master is expected tomorrow. Will pay to the 28th February.[10]

If Lincoln looked worn down, there was ample reason in the strain of heavy burdens borne by an unwarlike man in the midst of war. Still, his good nature flashed forth. Viewing a slim-looking bridge eighty feet high that had been hastily thrown across Potomac Creek by Union engineers, he called it a "beanpole and cornstalk" bridge.

The vagaries of the pay system are too mysterious
to understand; why pay in April should be only to the
end of February is impossible to fathom. The onset of
spring, with its promise of more solid footing, brought
expectations of an advance. "We are under marching
orders and may be off at any minute," wrote the major
on April 18:

> *The men have ten days' rations and one hundred and sixty*
> *rounds of Cartridges to carry. Are not permitted a single blan-*
> *ket, only their overcoats and one piece of shelter tent. This num-*
> *ber of rations will fill their Knapsacks as well as their*
> *Haversacks. We are not allowed any transportation. Even the*
> *Hospital wagons and Ambulances will be left behind. This looks*
> *as if Genl. Hooker expects a big fight without moving far. Sleep-*
> *ing on the ground this time of year without a single blanket*
> *will be pretty rough. I fear it will greatly increase the sick list.*
> *This campaign, I think, will be short but severe and decisive.*
> *One or both parties will be awfully used up. I visited Mrs. Genl.*
> *Graham last evening. She is a very agreeable lady. She has been*
> *sick for several days and as Dr. Jones went to Aquia I visited her*
> *for him. She rides a great deal on Horse back. She is quite pretty*
> *but like yourself [Emma] is afflicted with a superabundance of*
> *adipose tissue. I told her I had a letter from my Sister enquiring*
> *if a walk of several miles daily would not reduce her weight.*
> *She laughed heartily at the idea of walking only two or three*
> *miles. She said when at home she was accustomed to walk about*
> *ten miles every day. Said she would walk out here—but that*
> *the men stared at her so she disliked to go out. The rain we had*
> *a few days since raised the river about seven feet. This, I believe,*
> *is the reason we have not moved. They say Genl. Hooker swore*

all the day it rained. The Paymaster has not made his appearance. This is a great shame. He has the money and has been promising to come for the last month. On the 1st of May there will be six months' pay due us. The families of many of the soldiers are in a state of absolute destitution. You say Bedford is so dull you cannot find much to write about. Well, I bet it is not half as dull as our present old Camp.[11]

A private's family might easily become destitute on his pay of $13 a month when he did not get it for months. This sort of distress, however, did not trouble civilian profiteers, who waxed rich, as they generally do in wartime.

The Army of the Potomac, having packed up to move, did not move. Five days later, on April 23, the major wrote:

We have been prepared to move for several weeks but still we are here. A heavy rain set in last night and has continued incessantly ever since. The water is rapidly rising, rendering a big flood a sure thing. The roads will be so much impaired that it will be utterly impossible to move for one or two weeks. There is something wrong. . . . I am inclined to think the Authorities in Washington are fearful we shall be defeated if we cross the river in the vicinity of Fredericksburg and therefore do not exactly know what line of operations to pursue. If we are beaten there will be nothing to prevent the Enemy moving on Washington. Genl. Stoneman, with his Cavalry, was repulsed five times at Kelly's Ford. Had he succeeded in crossing we doubtless would have followed. Our delay may therefore be owing to his repulse or inability to find a suitable place for crossing. The rebel pickets are very defiant. Are continually inviting us or rather "bantering" us over. To successfully storm their fortifications, protected by the most effective modern Artillery and manned by a force equal if not superior to ours, is an impossibility. In a few weeks this Army will lose some twenty or thirty thousand troops, the two year and nine month men. Therefore it is the opinion of a great many that there will be no move till the Army is reorganized. Genl. Hooker certainly contemplated moving long before this—but something, probably known but to himself and the President, prevented. It was reported Hooker had resigned and Fremont was his successor. But no person credits this. . . . During the past week two soldiers of my Regt. cut off their right thumbs. Comment is unnecessary. These were accidental of course. Such cases were formerly discharged the service—but a recent order sends them to Genl. Hospital where they act in the capacity of nurses. This order will doubtless curtail this character of accidents. . . . I am weary of this place and hence am anxious for a move. I know almost every acre of ground in Stafford County. When we came here it seemed but one immense forest. Now scarcely a tree is visible. If the former inhabitants are ever permitted to return they will be unable to find a single familiar land mark. You cannot conceive how a country is devastated by an invading Army. When you ride out here you see nothing but a vast waste covered with white tents. An occasional House tumbling in ruins meets the eye—but presents no indication of a once happy home. I saw the other day a solitary Peach tree in blossom. It was a flame in the wilderness. How thankful we should be that grim war is not desolating the fair fields and happy homes of the North—and how unitedly and earnestly we should strive to sustain our glorious Union. How I despise those miserable traitors in the north who are aiding the rebels by calling every supporter of the administration Abolitionists. The time will come when patriots will glory in the name.

I would sooner be an abolitionist than a peace democrat—for the latter is the vilest thing on earth. . . . I have great trouble in getting up a letter—as there is nothing at all going on in this part of the world.[12]

*A*FTER STILL FURTHER DELAY, the advance began. On April 27, General John Sedgwick created a diversion by marching three corps to the Rappahannock east of Fredericksburg, the rest of the army remaining in camp preparatory to a fast move to Chancellorsville. Sedgwick would then take the enemy on his right flank while Hooker, with three and a half corps and Stoneman's cavalry, hit the left. On the 28th, the 1st Brigade of the 3rd Corps, including the 105th Pennsylvania, also marched to a point below Fredericksburg. "We moved day before yesterday," wrote the major on April 30,

> *and are now encamped about one quarter mile from the River on the North side. Genl. Hooker, with Heintzelman's and Stoneman's forces and the 2nd, 5th, 11th and 12th Corps, has crossed in the night. It is reported that he has been driving the rebels. So before the receipt of this you will have great news. Genl. Pleasonton is said to be killed. Genl. Sedgwick commands the left. Has three Corps—the 1st, 3rd and 6th. The 1st and 6th have crossed—and we may go over any moment. . . . The rain still continues with little prospect of clearing up. We are the reserves. I would much rather be in the advance as the Reserve is generally brought up just in the thickest of the fight and then remain the advance. We have been paid.[13]*

Hooker's confidence showed in a grandiose address to the army: "the operations of the last three days have determined that our enemy must ingloriously fly, or come out from behind their defences and give us battle on our own ground, where certain destruction awaits him." His plan was good, even to the choice of battlefield, high ground near Chancellorsville, about ten miles southwest of Fredericksburg. His army of 70,000, half again as large as Confederate forces, got over the river in good shape. But Lee was hardly a commander to fall in with any plan for "certain destruction." Scarcely heeding Sedgwick's diversion on his right, he concentrated against Hooker, only to be pushed back on May 1. Then, when Union troops seemed on the way to victory, Hooker, afflicted with disastrous loss of nerve, ordered a withdrawal, whereupon the enemy promptly moved up, and on May 2 renewed the battle in earnest. All might have gone well enough for Hooker had he not been deluded into believing that the day was won when Jackson marched off the field with 26,000 men. Jackson merely swung wide, then came roaring down so hard upon the Federal right that Sigel's 11th Corps crumpled in a rout that upset Hooker's whole army. It barely pulled itself together to check the enemy thrust, but that was all. Hooker could not regain the initiative.

Meanwhile Sedgwick, some distance removed, responded to urgent appeals from the commander by storming Marye's Heights behind Fredericksburg, and finally getting to the rear of Lee. But the two separated Union forces could effect no junction, nor could either take advantage of the enemy's hazardous position between. With great daring, Lee divided his army, then in two days of confused fighting, hammered Hooker on his front and Sedgwick in his rear until both were forced to retire.

It was a fearful four days. Union losses were more than 16,000 killed, wounded, and missing; Confederate, about 12,000. General Hooker was knocked out by a falling timber when a shell struck the Chancellor house. General Jackson was mortally wounded by one of his own sentries. During the night of May 5 the Union army, badly shaken by another defeat, began wearily recrossing the Rappahannock and marching back to its old camp near Falmouth. On that day Major Watson dispatched a hurried note:

> So far I am safe and well—have made some narrow escapes. We have had a most terrific fight. Have been fighting six days. Our Division, in fact the whole Corps, suffered terribly. Genl. Berry, commanding the 2nd Div., was killed and Genl. Whipple, commanding the 3rd, was wounded. We have lost two of our Div. Commanders. Our Brigade has not more than a Regt. and a half left. Col. McKnight was killed while gallantly leading a charge. The Rebels fought with the utmost desperation. The fight still continues. Last night the Rebels attacked our lines but were handsomely repulsed. Heavy cannonading is now heard in the direction of Fredericksburg. We are in the rear of this place. We were compelled to move Division Hospital five times—being shelled out. The first Hospital was knocked to pieces five minutes after we got out. I was under the heaviest kind of infantry fire once. Came near to losing my Horse. A shell killed a Horse tied next to him. . . . I have been operating a great deal. Don't know how many amputations I have performed. No Ambulances

and not permitted to cross the river to day—therefore I antici-
pate a big fight. Our loss so far in killed, wounded and missing
is almost thirty thousand—independent of the loss in front of
Fredericksburg. . . . Henry ran away when we retreated from
the first Hospital. Have not seen him since.[14]

The anticipated big fight did not occur. By this time all
the fight had been well beaten out of Fighting Joe Hooker.
The major's regiment returned to camp, from which he
wrote on May 7:

We returned to our old Camp last evening. The Rebels getting
the best of us we were compelled to retreat. The entire Army, so
far as I know, got over safely. There is nothing surprising in this
as we have had more experience in retreating than advancing. I
wrote you a few lines several days ago—and stated our loss was
about twenty thousand—fifteen, I believe, will cover it. The rebels
must have suffered more. I have been engaged every minute
since my return in making out Reports of the killed and
wounded. Our Regt. lost 91 men out of 330. I have just received
an order to have every thing in readiness to move at once. From
good authority I learn we will again cross the river. I am much
afraid we shall be again driven back. I came very near being
captured. The Rebels came on to one of our Hospitals five min-
utes after we got off. We lost 3 Medical Officers in our Brigade.
Don't know whether they are killed or prisoners. Many of the
Medical men behaved badly—ran off over the river in the first
day's fight and never came back at all.[15]

Whatever the intention of crossing the river to reopen
hostilities, Hooker, perhaps restrained by Halleck in
Washington, thought better of it. The Army of the Potomac remained in camp for the rest of the month. On the

8th the major wrote a fuller account of the Battle of Chancellorsville and its aftermath:

I understand Genl. Hooker intended recrossing the Rappahannock immediately in front of Fredericksburg—but the President refused to sanction the move. How true this is I am unprepared to say. But it is positively certain we will not remain idle long. . . . The recent fight was terrific beyond description. It was most admirably devised. Genl. Hooker secured just the position he desired and forced the enemy to attack him—and had it not been for the disgraceful and cowardly conduct of the 11th Army Corps would have gained a decided victory. But this Corps fled upon the approach of the enemy, many of the Regts. not firing a single shot. They lost the great part, if not all their Artillery. I know this to be true for I saw it myself. Our field Hospital was on the plank road ten miles south of Chancellorsville immediately in the rear of the 11th Corps. The advanced line of this Corps was distant almost a mile from our Hospital. Yet the Enemy were upon us twenty five minutes after they had fired the first Gun. A solid shot passed through the Hospital, which was a small log House, just as we left. When I took up my line of retreat I could distinctly see the Rebels advancing up the road and through the woods yelling like devils. The musket balls flew like hail. . . . About this time Henry ran off. He turned as near white as a Nigger possibly could, threw away his Knapsack, Haversack and all his effects and put off at lightning speed. I don't suppose he ever stopped till he recrossed the river. He returned yesterday after an absence of five days. I won't pay him in full for fear he will run off and go home. Genl. Berry's Div. of our Corps checked the rout. This was Saturday evening. The battle raged nearly the entire night. The roar of Cannon and rattle of Musketry exceeded any thing ever experienced. Officers who have been in many engagements say the Musketry exceeded any thing they ever experienced. At daylight Sunday morning the battle was renewed with increased fierceness. During the night we had strengthened our line by digging rifle pits, throwing up breastworks and massing our Batteries. The Rebels charged us six times and each time were repulsed with great slaughter. The carnage was fearful on both sides—Rebel loss much greater than ours as they could get but little of their Artillery in position on account of the woods. It was the most desperate fighting ever done on this continent. . . . On Sunday morning our Hospital was located in the woods behind our batteries. The Rebels opened on the Batteries and woods with grape, cannister and shell. It was the most frightful shelling ever I was in. The Battle of Fredericksburg was comparatively child's play. Thirty or forty shell were thrown right into us before we could get away. . . . To tell the truth I was considerably frightened. It requires a good deal of courage for a Surgeon to do his duty under such circumstances. I can say with a clear conscience I did mine. I don't profess to be very brave but I was always among the last to leave the Hospital and we were compelled to skedaddle five different times. I trust it may be a long time before I get into as hot a place again. Many of the Surgeons lost their Horses, instruments and every thing they had. I lost nothing but my sword and that was left by a Hospital Attendant who had it in charge. The 3rd Corps has immortalized itself. Did more fighting than any Corps in the Army. I am now speaking of the Army under the immediate control of Hooker. I don't know any thing about Sedgwick's fighting. But understand he was badly used up. Our Brigade especially covered itself with glory—lost over 700 men. The 141 Pa. lost 265 out of 419 and had more captured, but those wounded. Genl. Hooker on Sat-

urday night said the 3rd Corps had saved the Army. There is no doubt of it—and had it not been for this Corps our Army would have been driven into the Rappahannock. Had we occupied the position the Dutchman did the battle would have resulted differently. It won't do for the 11th Corps to talk about "fighting mit Sigel." They won't fight at all and are a burning disgrace to our Army. Capt. Kirk, the best Officer in our Regt. and my particular friend, was killed. He was shot through the head. We had three commissioned officers killed and quite a number wounded. It was a sad sight last evening to see our little Regt. on dress parade. Nearly one hundred familiar faces were missing. . . . Our Division was the last to leave the intrenchments. Had the Rebels discovered that we were retreating we would have had quite a serious time getting to the River. I heard this morning the Rebels skedaddled the same night we did. This accounts for us getting away so quietly and shows the Rebs were whipped as bad as we were. I trust Genl. Hooker will commence aggressive movements immediately. I want to see this war ended. And if they, notwithstanding our superiority in almost every thing, can whip us, why, let the world know it. They are certainly used up worse than we—and as we can raise 3 men to their one, why, let's go at them again and that immediately. The 2 year and 9 month men don't fight well. They thought if they could get out of this fight safely it would be their last—so they ran away. . . . The Medical staff of our Brigade, with several exceptions, behaved very creditably. Several of them went over the river on Sunday morning and never returned. They in all probability will be dismissed. We have had constant rain for four days. The weather is damp and cold. We had a pretty rough time lying out in the woods. My good clothes are completely ruined. Having no others, I was compelled to wear them.[16]

The major's spirit and his willingness to come to grips with the enemy were commendably aggressive. Perhaps he was rather severe in his judgment of Sigel's 11th Corps, which had been routed by Jackson's fierce charge. To give way, even panic, before the onrush of 26,000 determined, yelling "demons" might be, if not in the most sterling tradition of the veteran soldier, at least understandable.

As days went by without forward movement, the major became a little disgusted, but he tempered impatience by reflecting on the reoutfitting made necessary by losses at Chancellorsville. "We are still in the old Camp near Potomac Creek," he wrote his sister Charlotte on May 15,

> *living just as we were before the fight. We have drawn rations to the 1st June. But this indicates nothing. As an old campaigner I have discovered that it is impossible to predict a move. We never know when we are going till we are actually on the march. Therefore you know as well as I when the ensuing campaign will commence. We have just commenced to realize the extent of our disaster. . . . Twelve hundred of our wounded are still on the South side of the Rappahannock. Five of them belong to our Division. Genl. Lee will permit but two Ambulances and two Pontoon boats to be used in conveying them to our lines. It will require some days to bring them over with such limited transportation. This of course will give Lee plenty of time to reopen communications with Richmond. Genl. Sickles yesterday officially announced the death of Stonewall Jackson. His death will be a great loss to the Rebels. Our Corps will soon be in fighting trim again. Many of the Regts. required new Guns, Knapsacks*

and Haversacks. *Six thousand Knapsacks are required for our Corps alone. Every Army Corps has a badge to designate it. This badge is worn on the hat. Ours is a diamond. Red for the 1st Division, white for the 2nd and blue for the 3rd. After the fight on Sunday Genl. Hooker rode up to Genl. Sickles and said, "Well, Dan, Diamonds are trump to day." He could hardly have paid our Corps a higher compliment. Our Brigade went to the front on Friday afternoon and was sent on picket duty two and a half miles south of Chancellorsville. We remained there till 5 o'clock in the evening when we were ordered to the centre where the fighting was pretty brisk. Here we lost a few men from Artillery fire. Here I saw Genl. Hooker with his Staff ride through an open field to the scene of conflict. Shell were flying thick and fast. Without heeding them he rode on to the front where he directed the fight in person. He is a true soldier. Was at the front during the whole fight, day after day. While I admired his fear-less conduct I could not avoid thinking it wrong for the Com-manding General to expose himself so recklessly. I have not time nor do I care to tell you the position your humble servant occu-pied during [the] fight. It is sufficient to say I was in the front from Friday afternoon till Sunday afternoon, or in other words during all the heaviest fighting. I would rather have been more to the rear—and would have been had I consulted my own in-clination. . . . On Sunday afternoon we were ordered to estab-lish a Hospital near the River. Here I saw more Surgery than one would see in a whole lifetime of ordinary practice. . . . The Rebs with their shell and bullets were not the only enemies we were compelled to encounter during our short sojourn in the "Wilderness." The woods between Chancellorsville and the river are called the "Wilderness" by the Rebels. Wood ticks are the other enemies I allude to. The woods were alive with them. When they get under the skin it is next to an impossibility to get them out. I believe there are several in me yet. The weather is very warm. The last few days have turned me as brown as a berry. If I continue tanning in this same proportion I will soon be taken for a Contraband.*[17]

Hooker calmly riding to the front under fire exemplifies the personal bravery that was undoubtedly characteristic of all commanders of the Army of the Potomac. Yet some inability to think or act boldly in a crisis flawed his character, as similar shortcomings had hamstrung all other generals of this army. None so far had shown the tactical skill to make the Union superiority of numbers count in a decisive engagement. Perhaps all were intimidated by the great reputation of Lee and, up to this point, of his right arm, Jackson. Now Jackson was gone, as the major reported with fine restraint. He did not gloat over the death of this formidable adversary. In a letter to his father on May 17, he dwelt again on aspects of the great battle that, in the manner of soldiers, he called merely a "fight":

Dr. Ewing is in charge of the 2nd Div. (Hooker's old Division) Hospital. It is quite a responsible and important position and will relieve him from field duty. For my part I greatly prefer the latter. I belong to the Army and as long as I do so I intend accompanying my Regt. to the field of battle. Our missing Surgeons have all turned up—but I am sorry to say with very little honor. It is reported that with few exceptions they behaved most outrageously. It is said they were drunk almost the entire time, that they used the Stimulants sent over the River by the Medical

Director for our sick and that they shamefully neglected to dress the wounds of our own men. The Surgeons deny this, saying their supplies were too limited to do much good. It is very hard to get at the truth of the matter—so many conflicting statements are made. But one thing is certain, if they were drunk or negligent of the wounded they will suffer for it. I know myself many of the wounded who came to Division Hospital had not [had] their wounds dressed for six, some even for ten days—and that Erysipelas, Gangrene and Maggots resulted from this neglect. But who is to blame I know not. If the Surgeons are at fault, not only for the honor of the profession but for the sake of humanity I want to see them punished. I am truly thankful I was not captured—as I would not like to be identified with that party. There is an other class of non combatants I desire to say a word about. I refer to the Chaplains. Truth and justice compel me to say that with one or two exceptions all the Chaplains I have met are not only of no good or utility to the Army but a disgrace to the religion they profess. I have yet to see the 1st Chaplain ministering to either the spiritual or temporal wants of a wounded soldier. All they seem to care about is supplying themselves with rations and their horses with forage. I therefore consider Army Chaplains the rag tag and bobtail of the Ministry. I performed a great many and a great variety of operations during the last battle. I am now a very conservative Surgeon and will in future operate only when there is no possibility of saving a limb. . . . Quiet reigns supreme along the Rappahannock and both Armies occupy the same ground they did before the battle. From all appearances I don't think we will move soon. . . . My Horse is very sick. Don't know what is the matter with him. He looks as if he were going to make a die of it.[18]

*A*FTER A FEW LETTERS chiefly about family matters, the major returned to camp and army themes on May 26:

> We will change Camp in a few days—as the Regts. are too close
> for health. Will move but a short distance, not over a mile at
> most. The news from Grant is most cheering. I do hope it is
> true. The papers told so many falsehoods about the Chancellors-
> ville fight that I am inclined to give very little credence to any
> thing except the official Reports. Newspaper correspondents, I
> find, have but little regard for the truth. They subsist by letter
> writing—and hence write any thing to make a letter. But as the
> Rebels admit Grant's success there can be no doubt of it. I only
> wish we were in condition to strike an other blow for the Union.
> Our Army is so much diminished that I fear we will have to
> stand on the defensive till reinforced.[19]

General Grant, aided by William Sherman, James McPherson, and Admiral David Dixon Porter's fleet of gun-boats, had been doggedly working along the Mississippi River toward Vicksburg. Finding the town impregnable to direct assault, on May 18, he began to invest the place with a ring of besieging trenches and battery emplacements. An officer who had come up out of nowhere, Grant was showing the tenacity that within a year would move him up to full command of all Union armies. His success was indeed cheering to the administration and to the punch-drunk Army of the Potomac. Still, though Hooker's bat-tered troops were "much diminished," action was not far off, for even as the major wrote, Lee was preparing for an invasion of Pennsylvania.

For about three weeks longer, however, all seemed peaceful along the Rappahannock. "I would have writ-ten you sooner," wrote the major to his father on June 4, *but I have been constantly employed the past few days in moving camp and preparing my monthly Reports. Dr. Sims is so very particular about the Reports that it requires a great deal of time and labor to get them up neatly and correctly. My last report was both difficult and tedious to make out. I was compelled to report in detail the seat and character of all wounds—the different operations performed and their results. Moving Camp is no small matter. In addition to attending to my own Quarters I am required to select a site for my Hospital and to superintend its arrangement. . . . I have lost but one case from disease since I was at home. That was a case of Pernicious fever and died before any thing could be done. Our present Camp is located near the mouth of Potomac Creek—or rather near Belle Plain landing. . . . We have splendid air and good water— but I fear we are too near the Bay for health. Immediately in the rear of the Camp there is a large marsh about a mile in extent. My Hospital is situated on a small bluff overhanging this swamp. The tide submerges the greater portion of the marsh every morning. This may prevent vegetable decomposition and consequently the generation of miasmatic fever. Still I don't like this swamp. With this exception I prefer it to any Camp we have yet occupied. It will be an awful place for Mosquitoes, though. . . . it is rumored Lee intends coming over. Hooker is watching Lee very closely. It is said Lee is massing his forces at Chancellorsville. Our Army, though greatly weakened, is strong enough to whip Lee should he attack us. If he comes over he will be compelled to fight on open ground. He can't afford to do that even if he were sure of success—for in a fair open fight he would lose too many men. For my part I wish he would come over. I think we could whip him this side of the river. If we can't, let him whip us. I don't think it would make it worse than now—for as long as we kill as many of them as they of us we are getting the advantage of them. We can afford to lose more men than they. If Lee don't assume the offensive I don't think Hooker will disturb him—as it would be folly for Hooker to cross without reinforcements. . . . Dr. Loty has been appointed Surgeon of the 14th Congressional district to superintend the conscription. I was not aware before his appointment that Surgeons in the field were detailed for this duty. I would like very much to spend the Summer North. I would not have a Hospital—but would like extremely well to have a district. I suppose all the appointments have been made by this time. Still you may inquire and if there is any chance I would like you to attend to it for me. The Secretary of war is the only person, I believe, who has the power to detail Surgeons from the field on this duty. This would be only temporary—as I would rejoin my Regt. as soon as the conscription was finished. . . . The Regt. is on picket. Went out this morning. I could not leave my sick— but will ride out every day and see how they are getting along. They are stationed about 8 or 10 miles from here on the Warrenton road.[20]*

The major's dream of spending a summer in the north as supervisor of conscription was a pleasant fantasy that evaporated when the enemy began to move. "The rebels," he wrote on June 5,

are said to be crossing in force on our right. There has been some skirmishing on the Picket lines. I presume some of the good people of old Penna., are fearfully expecting a visit from Genl. Lee. They need not be alarmed if the Pennsylvanians will fight as well at home as they do in the Army. Our Brigade is composed entirely of Penna. Regiments. In the battle of Chan-

cellorsville the Brigade lost 750 out of 1900 and is admitted to
have done the hardest fighting of any troops in the Corps. Penna.
troops fight better than the New Yorkers.[21]

At this time the 1st Brigade, commanded by Brigadier
General Charles K. Graham, was composed of the 57th,
63rd, 68th, 105th, 114th, and 141st Pennsylvania. Major
Watson's boast about the fighting qualities of Pennsylvania troops was well founded. Of fifty Union regiments
suffering the highest percentage of casualties, a statistic
cited as a gauge of stamina, twelve were from Pennsylvania, more than twice the number from any other state.
The major showed a proper pride in his outfit. The veteran soldier jealously defended the good name of his
corps, his brigade and regiment. Men of the same unit
developed a clan spirit that, if sometimes edgy and quar-
relsome, grew from comradeship on the march, around
campfires, in battle lines hazardous with the imminence
of sudden death. As days went by, the hint of something
momentous in the air became more pronounced. "On
Friday afternoon," said the major on June 9,

> *a portion of Sedgwick's Corps crossed the River below Fredericks-*
> *burg. The cannonading was heavy—our loss about sixty. Genl.*
> *Robinson with his Division is also over. Genl. Hooker, I think,*
> *merely intends a reconnaissance to ascertain if the enemy is*
> *still in force at Fredericksburg—or possibly as a feint to prevent*
> *Lee reinforcing Vicksburg. The entire Army is under marching*
> *orders—but it don't look as much like a move now as several*
> *days ago. I don't think Hooker cares to bring on a general en-*
> *gagement. He has the whole Army in fighting condition in or-*
> *der to be prepared for any emergency. I now hear pretty heavy*

cannonading on the right and as the marching orders have not been countermanded we may be off at any moment. . . . Since we changed Camp the health of the Regt. is most excellent. I have not had a single new case of miasmatic fever. We have a delightful breeze both day and night. I must confess I am most agreeably disappointed for when I first came here I feared it was a very unhealthy location. We are encamped on an open plain but have secured plenty of shade by planting pine and cedars around our Quarters. . . . This morning at "Surgeon's Call" Dr. Wenger refused to excuse a fellow who is in the habit of "playing off." He was highly exasperated and started off muttering and growling. Wenger took hold of him and asked him what he was saying. He replied, "Well, if you won't excuse me I will go to the old man." I am often amused at them calling me the "old man" and the "old Doctor." . . . I have been paid to the 1st May. It amounted to $320. I sent you $220, all I could conveniently spare. I bought some Clothes, paid my expenses to this date and have about seventy dollars left. Lieut. Nesbit. . . . was dismissed the Service for having Col. Craig's official report of the battle of Chancellorsville published in the Phila. Enquirer. . . . It merely stated the part our Regt. took in the action and gave a tabular statement of the casualties. Genl. Birney had it done. Nesbit was a good and brave Officer and it was a great shame to dismiss him for so trivial an offense. . . . You must excuse this letter as I had nothing interesting to write.[22]

*E*ARLY IN JUNE LEE STARTED NORTH, crossed the Potomac, and on the 13th concentrated his army at Hagerstown, Maryland. Three days later the Confederates were near Chambersburg, headed for the Pennsylvania capital. Alarm spread. Lincoln issued a proclamation that stressed the danger to Maryland, Pennsylvania, West Virginia, and Ohio, and called for 100,000 militia from those states to repel invasion. In Baltimore, makeshift citizen soldiery barricaded streets with tar barrels and sugar hogsheads. At Pittsburgh, merchants and mechanics formed military companies to defend the city. Harrisburg throbbed with excitement and confusion, the chaos aggravated by the arrival of wagon trains from the broken division of General Milroy, who had been routed by Richard Ewell at Winchester, Virginia. McConnellsburg, Shippensburg, York, and Carlisle were overrun. Washington was in a panic when Stuart's cavalry swooped to within thirteen miles of the city.

Meanwhile, Hooker, somewhat belatedly sensing the enemy's intentions, had started the Army of the Potomac on a fast march northward via a route east of, but parallel to, that of the Army of Northern Virginia, Federal forces keeping between the invaders and Washington. In the midst of this march Hooker, because of an altercation with Halleck over withdrawing troops from Harper's Ferry, asked to be relieved of command. "Impressed," said he, "with the belief that my usefulness as the commander of the army of the Potomac is impaired, I part from it, yet not without the deepest emotion." Into this perilous situation, while the Union army headed for what looked like a showdown fight, stepped a new commander on June 28, Major General George Gordon Meade.

The danger to the North prompted a diatribe from Major Watson on June 24:

I see by the paper that the Rebels have been all around you— being in Cumberland, Fulton Co., and Hancock—and that Genl. Milroy is at Bloody Run. His presence, I presume, will be a sufficient protection for Bedford and County. His forces must be terribly demoralized to run all the way from Winchester to Bloody Run. From all accounts they made but feeble resistance to the rebel invaders. I only wish our little Brigade was in Bedford County and I venture to say they would not devastate it with impunity. . . . It is most disgraceful for loyal Pennsylvanians to permit a handful of Rebels to ride without resistance wherever they please. Why don't the people rise and drive them from the State? It is most discouraging to this Army to know that Pennsylvania with her thousands of able bodied men has not fired a single shot at the enemy. Do they expect the Army of the Potomac to do every thing? This Army is now holding Lee in check. If it were not so he would devastate the fair fields of Penna. and seize our National Capitol. It appears there has only been a few Guerrillas in Pennsylvania and still they have been permitted to ride at pleasure wherever they choose. I blush for Pennsylvania. Here we are surrounded on all sides by Guerrillas. They burned day before yesterday three wagons within a few hundred yards of our picket line. Genl. Birney, while riding out, was fired at and pursued almost into Camp. Thirteen of the Guerrillas were captured. Genl. Pleasonton defeated Stuart on Sunday near Aldie. The Cavalry is beginning to do good service. The paper states that bouquets were presented the Rebs at McConnellsburg. This is very encouraging to an army who have traveled Va. for two years without ever receiving a smile from a Lady. I tell you, Pa, if the people in the north do not give up bitter political feeling, unite and exhibit a more patriotic and energetic spirit we might as well give up the struggle. Look at the difference. They ride through Penna. without molestation— while we cannot go a hundred yards outside of the picket line without being fired at.[23]

Irony may be suspected in the major's endorsement of Milroy as an adequate protector. Commanding two brigades, he had been so precipitously ousted from Winchester by a surprise attack that his flight brought him before a court of inquiry. Milroy explained that the defeat occurred because of improper execution of orders, but his military reputation, none too brilliant at best, fell under a cloud that remains to this day. The affair at Aldie, Virginia, on June 21, was a sharp four-hour encounter between some five Union cavalry regiments and Stuart's advance troopers. Pleasonton's success in forcing the enemy to withdraw showed, as the major said, that Union horsemen were improving.

When the armies clashed at Gettysburg on July 1 to 3, the violent tides of conflict took a ghastly toll: on both sides more than 50,000 killed, wounded, or missing. The 105th Pennsylvania was in the thick of the fight. On July 2 it advanced with the 3rd Corps, under General Daniel E. Sickles, to the peach orchard almost a mile beyond the Union line. Though reinforced by the 2nd and 5th Corps, this exposed force was so badly battered by Ambrose Hill and Longstreet that it had to fall back, Birney having assumed command when Sickles was knocked over by a serious wound that cost him a leg. The small 105th lost heavily: its casualties for the terrible three days were 132. The unfortunate 11th Corps, abused for its flight at Chancellorsville, collapsed again on July 1, though it did not panic this time.

Major Watson was not with his regiment in the peach orchard but rather either at division hospital or at the 3rd Corps hospital on high ground near the Schwartz house. Not until several days after the battle did he find time for a brief note. On July 7 he wrote:

> *I am safely through the most desperate conflict I ever witnessed. My Regiment suffered most severely, losing one half. Col. Craig had two horses shot under him. One was shot eleven times. Wat is here. Several of his men were wounded and just at our hospital. So you may know the firing was close. I never was and never wish to be in such a shower of solid shot and shell. The house and barn occupied as a hospital were completely riddled. Of course we were compelled to fall back; in doing so a solid shot passed within a few feet of the mare's head. She threw herself flat on the ground, did not hurt me. I never had so many operations. Day before yesterday I performed fourteen amputations without leaving the table. I do not exaggerate when I say I have performed at the least calculation fifty amputations. There are so many severely wounded through the joints. There are many operations yet to be performed. The surgeons, except those detailed to operate here, have rejoined their Regts. as Genl. Meade intends closely following up his victory. I am detailed as operator for the Division. . . . Most of [the wounded] are lying on the wet ground without any shelter whatever. The people in this district have done nothing for them. I have yet to see the first thing brought in for the comfort of the wounded. Some farmers brought in some bread which they sold for seventy five cents a loaf. The brave army that has protected this State surely de-*

*serves better treatment. . . . I do not know how long I will be
retained here, not longer I presume than we can send off all the
wounded. I trust so anyhow as I am anxious to be with my
Regiment. Did not wish to stay but the Medical Director would
not let me off.*[24]

The major's matter-of-fact report of operations performed
recalls those grisly drawings of piles of severed arms and
legs near field hospitals, in full view of lines of wounded
men waiting their turn to go under the knife. Meade's
expected pursuit of the retreating Confederates turned
out to be only a feeble gesture, to the great chagrin of
Lincoln, who had hoped for a knockout blow. But the
badly mauled Union army was scarcely in the best condition to deliver a telling stroke, and Lee got back to Virginia without serious hindrance. If Meade's failure to
follow up his not very decisive victory caused disappointment in Washington, it was partly offset by the surrender of Vicksburg to Grant on July 4. Three days later,
when Port Hudson fell, the Mississippi River was in
Union hands, again flowing, in Lincoln's words, "un-
vexed to the sea."

Major Watson remained on hospital duty at
Gettysburg for two months or more. "I am so very busy,"
he wrote on July 9,

*that I have time to write but a few lines. We have eight hundred
wounded in our Div. Hospital and only eight Medical Officers to
attend them. The most pleasing feature in this battle is that we
were able to get all our wounded off the field. The past few days
I have been doing the operating for the whole Division. . . . I
still have a few operations in my own Division when I will turn*

my attention to wounded Rebels. There are about one hundred of them in a Barn near us in a most distressing condition. Many of them require operating. Old Army Surgeons say the wounds are more serious and amputations more numerous in this than any previous battle. I had six amputations above the knee in one company of the 141st Pa. Vols. I performed two shoulder and one knee joint operations—all doing well. I can say without egotism that I have made quite a reputation as an operator even among army Surgeons. All the slightly wounded are being sent off—it is impossible to remove the serious cases. Dr. Letterman, I understand, intends establishing a general Hospital in Gettysburg. This will consolidate all the Corps Hospitals. I presume I will remain here till this is accomplished. . . . From all accounts Genl. Lee is in a most unpleasant situation. He certainly will lose the greater part of his army before crossing the Potomac. . . . Genl. Meade handled the army splendidly— and the army never fought more gallantly. Our Corps fought on the left flank and on Thursday sustained the combined attack of Hill's, Ewell's and a portion of Longstreet's Corps. Meade reinforced just in time. On Friday we had it all our own way, giving Lee the most complete whipping he ever received. Genl. Dix, instead of being before Richmond, is at Culpeper. So Lee will have Heintzelman, Dix, French and the Army of the Potomac to encounter before he escapes. This, with the capture of Vicksburg, renders me sanguine that the end is near at hand. I conversed with a Rebel Officer yesterday. He said Lee would get back into Virginia without sacrificing his army or disparaging his own reputation. I confess "I can't see it." I never was in such a miserable country in my life. Can get nothing to eat or nothing to feed my Horse. Have been without forage for five days. I had my pack horse stolen. My mare, in addition to the distemper, is lame. So I am rather unfortunate in regard to Horseflesh.[25]

Notwithstanding such an impressive aggregation as Generals Heintzelman, John A. Dix, and William H. French, not to speak of the Army of the Potomac, no massing of forces prevented Lee from crossing the river on July 13 and getting away without loss of his army. The major's hopes of a speedy end to the war were to be delayed of fulfillment for almost two years. Gettysburg soon became a tourist attraction. "Hundreds of people from all parts of the Country have been here," he wrote on July 18:

> *There were thirty or forty persons from Hollidaysburg. But no person, as far as I know, from Bedford. I really thought there were persons in Bedford who would like to have seen a Battle field. . . . I have performed the greatest number and variety of operations. Have ligated the Carotid Femoral and Brachial Arteries and resected and amputated every bone in the body leading [?] to such operations. . . . Before the fight our Brigade numbered over fifteen hundred—now scarcely five. The mortality among the wounded is fearful—caused principally by Gangrene, Erysipelas, Tetanus and Secondary Hemorrhage. Our secondary operations have been very unfavorable. Most of the cases die. . . . I am sorry Lee escaped without an other fight. But we in the Army know how easy it is for one Army to give an other the slip. It is very difficult to force an Army to fight when the Commanding Genl. wishes to avoid it. I was off duty yesterday—being completely exhausted. To day I am perfectly well. . . . It is hard to be so near home and not see any person I know. I have been here since the 1st July.*[26]

Two days later he wrote again:

> *My Hospital is located just in the rear of the place our Corps fought. This was on the extreme left of the line—about 3 miles from Gettysburg. Dr. Hildreth, Surgeon in charge of Corps Hospital, thinks we will remain about 8 or 10 days longer. I am still very busy, though not so much so as a few days since. You say you will send me something to eat. I get plenty now—therefore do not require it. But when we first came here I was nearly starved. Had nothing but two hard crackers for 3 days. You seem to be much disappointed that Lee's Army was not bagged or annihilated. It is totally impossible to do either with so large an army as Lee's. Both at Fredericksburg and Chancellorsville we were right in front of the Enemy. Still we stole off in the night without molestation. It is a very hazardous thing to bring on an engagement in the night. As many men are killed on our side as on the Enemy's.*[27]

How long Major Watson remained on hospital duty near Gettysburg is uncertain. A gap of over two months occurs in the letters here. The pull of home, about seventy miles away, must have been too strong to resist, for at some point he went over the hill to visit Bedford without permission, but suffered no official reproof for this unmilitary act. During the summer the Army of the Potomac moved south, but except for sporadic cavalry clashes did not meet the enemy in an all-out fight. When the major wrote again on September 27, he was with his regiment in camp near Culpeper, Virginia:

> *I can't understand why I have not received the very many letters written from home. Several of our Officers say that some of*

their letters have been sent to the 103rd Pa. Vols. in North Caro-
lina—the Postmaster mistaking a 3 for a 5. This may be the
solution of the mystery. . . . Quiet reigns supreme here at present.
But we all feel rather depressed at Rosecrans' defeat. The 11th
and 12th Corps have left here. They were ordered to report to
Genl. Hooker in Alexandria. The impression here is they go to
reinforce Rosecrans. I understand the 1st and 2nd Corps will
also go. This will leave but 3 Corps in the Army of the Potomac,
the 3rd, 6th and 5th. So this Army is not likely to make an
advance at present. I think this right—for the possession of
Chattanooga is of much greater importance than Richmond.
. . . The nights are mighty cold and as we have no stoves the
evenings are by no means the most pleasant part of the day.[28]

In Georgia, Rosecrans, commanding the Army of the
Cumberland, was outmaneuvered by Bragg, who soundly
defeated the Federals at Chickamauga on September 19–
20. Rosecrans's army escaped disaster only by the stub-
born resistance of Major General George H. Thomas, commanding the Union left. While broken Federal brigades
fled toward Chattanooga, he covered the wild retreat by
holding Horseshoe Ridge against determined assaults,
thus earning the sobriquet of "The Rock of Chickamauga." Under cover of night he withdrew to Chattanooga, where the Union army would soon be under siege
and come near starving. Total casualties of more than
33,000 at Chickamauga made it one of the bloodiest
battles of the war.

Another gap ensues in the major's correspondence.
After three weeks he wrote from Fairfax Station, Virginia,
on October 18:

I have experienced some very rough times recently. We marched from Culpeper here, a distance of more than 70 miles, in three days. It is the most famous march of the war—for we brought all our trains with us and were compelled to fight or rather skirmish the entire route. The Brigade had quite a spirited little fight at Auburn. Our Regt. lost about ten. I saw the famous Cavalry fight at Brandy Station. Our Division supported Genl. Pleasonton. Several charges were made before the Rebels gave way. The last charge was terrific, scattering the Rebs in every direction. It was a glorious sight. . . . The Rebels fired into our columns throughout the entire march. Sometimes I began to think my chance for seeing old Bedford again mighty slim. Col. Craig is in command of this Post and I am Post Surgeon. . . . [Unable to finish this letter because of another march, he completed it at a camp near Catlett's Station on October 21.] I did not get time to conclude my letter the other day for we received orders to pack up without delay and in an hour's time were again on the march. Truly there is no rest for the wicked. We arrived at this place to day. So we are again but a few miles from the Rappahannock. Why Genl. Meade retreated to the fortifications without giving battle I don't pretend to say for the very good reason that I don't know. But I do pretend to say that had he fought them he could easily have beaten them, save thousands [of] dollars of Uncle Sam's property, and very probably prevented Lee from reinforcing Bragg. The Rail Road from Bristoe Station to Rappahannock is completely destroyed. Not a tie or rail or Bridge remains. You never saw a road more thoroughly gutted. Even the abutments have been blown up. It will take at least a week, if not more, to repair the road. The most unpleasant part of the business is that the Rebels, when we advanced, declined to fight and have all recrossed the Rappa-

hannock. From what I have stated you will naturally conclude it was a strange move we made. So it was. It possibly may have been strategic—but I can't see it. We will be apt to remain here till the road is fixed. After that, time alone can enable me to say what this Army will do. I am truly thankful the Penna. and Ohio elections went so strong for the Union.[29]

The major's perplexity over Meade's movements is understandable. The commander was maneuvering, trying to feel out the enemy without at the moment bringing on a general engagement. Lee seemed equally reluctant to give battle. Hence the armies marched and countermarched, and collided only in minor skirmishing. The fight at Brandy Station was a brush with a dismounted detachment of Stuart's cavalry. Union troopers, horses galloping and sabers flashing in a traditional charge, no doubt made an exhilarating display.

Camp life was certainly not comfortable, but the major was not a whiner. Still, there is nostalgic longing for the pleasures of home in his letter to his sister Marie on November 19:

You say I must come home during the Holidays. I can assure you, my dear Sis, nothing in the world would give me greater pleasure. . . . Leaves of absence will not be granted till we go into Winter Quarters and this will not be before an other fight. The railroad is completed to Brandy Station and the troops are being supplied with clothing as rapidly as possible. We have marching orders with twenty days' rations—and in a very few days will again take up our line of march and offer battle to the rebs who occupy a strong and well fortified position on the Rapidan. The war department, I presume, expects us to winter in

Richmond. At all events a forward move is certain—but time alone can develop its results. Many a good soldier, I fear, will go to his long rest before this campaign ends—but this, if we are successful, is a small matter. When you are sitting by your comfortable stoves or in your good and warm old fashioned Pa. bed think . . . of your absent brother by his silent and not too comfortable camp fire.[30]

After a short break, Major Watson wrote on November 24:

Reveille sounded this morning at 4 o'clock with orders to be ready to march at 7. So we struck tents, saddled horses, loaded our baggage (fortunately I am not troubled with any of the latter commodity), and then, after standing several hours in a cold rain impatiently awaiting orders to fall in and forward march, were notified that the movement had been postponed for the present in consequence of the rain. Of course we were well satisfied—but felt rather wrothy the countermanding orders had not been sent before we had taken down our quarters. If Genl. Meade did not intend fighting I don't think he would permit inclement weather to delay him. He will not be compelled to go far if it be true the Rebs are in force on the Rapidan. It is said by some the Genl. intends going to the White House on the Peninsula—by others that he contemplates a flank movement via Fredericksburg—while others say he will cross the Rapidan immediately in front of his present position. The truth is, however, no one with the exception probably of his Corps Commanders know where he is going or what he intends doing and this, to my mind, is one of the very best indications of success. . . . By the way, I think Pa should write me, at least occasionally. I am not fonder of letter writing than himself and yet because I think it affords him and you Girls some slight plea-

*sure or at least relieves you of anxiety I flood you with my hasty
and uninteresting letters.[31]*

A few days later five army corps, including the major's,
and two cavalry divisions crossed the Rapidan and
marched into the Wilderness. In a brief campaign of
about a week this force met segments of the Army of
Northern Virginia, and lost some 1,500 men in encounters at Mine Run, Raccoon Ford, New Hope, Robertson's
Tavern, Bartlett's Mills, and Locust Grove. By early December Union troops had returned to camp near Brandy
Station. On the 4th Major Watson wrote a summary of
operations:

*After a rough but brief Campaign in the "wilderness" I again
find myself in the old Camp near Brandy Station. The 3rd Corps
left this place on Thanksgiving day morning and with the 6th
Corps crossed the Rapidan at Jacob's Ford where we bivouacked
for the night. Early next morning we took up our line of march
for Robertson's Tavern where we were to form a junction with
the 2nd Corps. Genl. Prince, commanding the 2nd Division of
our Corps, had the advance. Missing the road he ran into the
enemy's line near Orange Grove—where a brisk fight ensued.
The 2nd and 3rd Divisions were driven back some five or six
hundred yards when the gallant old 1st Div. went in on a charge
and completely routed the enemy. They fled in confusion, leaving their dead and wounded on the field. I never heard fiercer
Musketry. In consequence of the thickness of the woods it was
impossible to use much Artillery. It is truly and literally a "wilderness"—for miles and miles you see nothing but an impen-
etrable forest of pines and ground oaks. . . . Saturday morning
it rained and in a few hours the roads were almost impassable.*

. . . *Roads, when wet and tramped over by thousands of troops, Horses and Artillery, soon become very bad and hard to travel. In the evening we reached Mine Run, upon the west side of which the enemy were strongly entrenched. The weather was intensely cold and had a battle been fought, hundreds of poor fellows would inevitably have frozen to death. Genl. Meade ordered the attack to commence Monday morning at 8 o'clock. He sent Genl. Warren with 2nd Corps, the 2nd and 3rd Divs. of the 3rd Corps, and one Div. of the 6th, to turn the enemy's right flank. In accordance with orders, at 8 o'clock our Division opened on the enemy and advancing drove them out of their first line of rifle pits. But Genl. Birney, having no support and seeing the rest of the line was not advancing, ordered the rifle pits to be abandoned. Had the rest of the army advanced, our Division might have carried the works on their front easily. Genl. Warren, it seems, found the enemy's position on the right impregnably fortified and, deeming it suicidal to attack, returned to his former position. And this is the reason the Army of the Potomac did not have an other big fight. The enemy's position was so strong that had we attacked we would almost certainly have been repulsed. Prince, by mistaking the road, delayed our Corps two entire days. . . . This of course gave the enemy time to fortify a very strong natural position. But to say the least of the "wilderness," it is a mighty ugly locality and I am truly glad to be well out of it. Wednesday night we "dusted," as the Boys say, over the river. We "double quicked" for five miles. I have not slept a wink for three nights. . . . The long roll beat last night just as I was getting into bed. We were compelled to pack up every thing. The wagons came for our tents and in about one hour we were ready for action. After waiting almost all night orders were received stating the emergency was over and the troops might make themselves comfortable. We were called out to form a line as the enemy had crossed the Rapidan—but Genl. Warren, I understand, with our Cavalry defeated them with considerable loss. I have been engaged all day making out my monthly reports—and having no sleep and no rest for several days and nights am completely used up. I was never so tired in all my life as this evening. . . . If our Regt. don't get any conscripts (and I don't think it will) it will be mustered out about the 1st of next September. I will be mustered out with it—so you can look for me by next fall and if the war ends before that, sooner. . . . I was a great fool for parting with the Mare. She is now in North Carolina. I wish you would look me up a good stylish horse—one not too large. I don't care for the gait—and if I am fortunate enough to get a furlough I will buy him and bring him down with me. The horse I have does very well—but is rather too unsteady on his pins for safety.*[32]

$\mathcal{T}$HE MAJOR WAS GLAD to get out of the Wilderness, but fortunately he did not know that within five months he would be there again with Grant's army. In the momentary calm, he wrote on December 13:

The weather is most delightful—just like April and today is the anniversary of my first experience of actual warfare—the battle of Fredericksburg—but the Army, in place of reenacting this fearful drama, is quietly and busily engaged making comfortable quarters for the winter. Furloughs for ten days are now being granted. I put in for one this morning. It will return in 4 or 5 days—but whether it will return approved is an other ques-

tion. There are a great many Surgeons from our Division applying and as the Medical Director of the Corps has been informed I took a "french leave" while at Gettysburg and remarked that when furloughs were granted he would remember those Medical Officers who went home from there I am, I must confess when I think of it, a little doubtful of the result. Still I have been a pretty good fellow (even if I do say it myself) and therefore entertain very sanguine anticipations of getting home. I always endeavor to look on the bright side and so I won't despair till my leave is actually disapproved. . . . Ten days are certainly not much—but a soldier receives them with more thanks and greater delight than a schoolboy his summer vacation. Wat paid me two visits lately. . . . He had eaten nothing but Army rations for two weeks. My larder being pretty well stocked, I was able to feed him pretty well for the army. I had Bread and butter—Apples, Lobster, Canned fruits and so forth and after feasting a day or so I sent him on his way rejoicing.[33]

The year of 1863 faded out without further decisive action by the Army of the Potomac as it settled into winter quarters. Whether or not Major Watson got his leave is not clear. His correspondence, interrupted by a break of two months, does not resume until February 1864.

1864

ℰARLY IN FEBRUARY 1864, the 105th Regiment, and doubtless other units, were sent to Pennsylvania. Possibly the trip was one of those morale-raising displays, like the bond rallies of World War I. Major Watson had chided Pennsylvanians for sluggish lack of patriotism. Perhaps Governor Curtin also believed that the home folks might be stimulated by the presence of their own veteran regiments. On February 10, General Meade made a short speech in Philadelphia, and probably some of his troops were there too. On the day after, Major Watson and his regiment were on the other side of the state, in Pittsburgh, he having arrived there separately from his outfit. From that city he wrote on February 11:

> I arrived here safely yesterday noon. Camp Copeland is distant 9 miles from the City. In all probability I will report there this afternoon. I fortunately met the Colonel and so avoided going to Camp by reporting to him in the City. . . . The Colonel says we will return to the Army of the Potomac but don't know how

soon. . . . Acting upon your advice I called for a "Jack Salmon."
It was decidedly the finest fish I ever ate.[1]

It is pleasant to see the major, like other soldiers temporarily released from camp life, making the most of city
advantages when he had them. Whatever the purpose
of this junket, it lasted about ten days, after which he
and others rejoined the Army of the Potomac near Culpeper, Virginia. "We arrived at our present Camping
ground day before yesterday," he wrote on February 23,

> *and are busily engaged constructing quarters. We are located*
> *between Brandy Station and Culpeper—about three miles from*
> *the latter place. Our Camp is on a hill in a large pine woods*
> *with plenty of wood and water convenient. Altogether it is one*
> *of the best sites for a Camp I have ever seen. I have no tent—*
> *mine having been condemned and turned in when we went*
> *north. I expect a new one to day or tomorrow. We were a long*
> *time getting here in consequence of the difficulty in procuring*
> *transportation—and the Officers, having no tents or shelter, were*
> *compelled to stop at the Hotels. The delays were pleasant but*
> *very expensive. It cost me over a hundred dollars to get here. I*
> *am now going to be very economical—will subsist entirely upon*
> *government rations for at least four months in order to make*
> *up for the extravagance of the past two. In order to see the Girls*
> *I obtained the Colonel's permission to leave Harrisburg for Bal-*
> *timore before the Regt. Unfortunately the train was delayed and*
> *instead of getting in at 5 o'clock did not get there till after 10*
> *o'cl. The Regt. came in at 12 o'cl. the same night and the Colo-*
> *nel sent me word he would leave for Washington at 10 in the*
> *morning. I therefore had but an hour or two with the Girls.*

. . . I have a good deal of business this afternoon and besides there is a Division review and our Regt. is ordered to attend. Henry is with me safe enough. He looks pretty blue. This may be owing to his whisky ration being stopped. . . . Please send me some stamps.[2]

$\mathcal{F}$OR SOME TIME in battle-scarred Virginia the Army of the Potomac engaged in only desultory action, chiefly reconnaissance patrols by the cavalry commands of Generals George A. Custer and Judson Kilpatrick, aided by infantry. On March 3 the major wrote:

Our Division returned yesterday from a five days' reconnaissance. I was not along, not being very well. . . . There is nothing of interest transpiring in this Army. Last Sunday the 6th Corps, in conjunction with our Division, advanced to Thoroughfare Mountain for the purpose of supporting the Cavalry which had crossed the Rapidan. But for what purpose or with what results I am unable to say. Our Regt. has just returned with a great many sick. The weather was inclement and the march long and fatiguing and many of them had neither gum blankets or shelter. I did not accompany the Regt. as I was suffering with rather a severe bronchial attack. Of this I have entirely recovered. But on waking up on Tuesday morning I was quite surprised to find myself unable to use my right arm and left leg. Since then I have been confined to bed. It is something like inflammatory Rheumatism. . . . The disease has more of the characteristics of sub acute than inflammatory Rheumatism and therefore I expect to be all right in a few days. . . . Don't be at all alarmed or uneasy about me for I have very snug Quarters, and

Rheumatism, although a very painful, is not a dangerous affliction.[3]

If Major Watson seemed more war-weary than usual, there was reason. The two armies sat there, Confederates entrenched south of the Rapidan, Federals encamped north of it, both glumly shivering in the raw spring weather. Perhaps the major used his illness as a means to get a furlough, which he spent at home, also visiting friends in Philadelphia. Evidently he enjoyed himself, for he overstayed his leave by two days, but he was not hauled to the guardhouse for this breach of discipline. "I arrived here safely yesterday afternoon," he wrote from camp on April 6,

> *two days after time. The Colonel said my certificate was neither sufficient nor in accordance with regulations—but that so far as he was concerned no notice would be taken of it. He has reported me all along absent by proper authority. Therefore I apprehend no further difficulty in the matter. The Colonel endeavored to impress very strongly on me that my escaping so easily was in a great measure due to my efficiency as a Medical Officer and his friendship. I entered upon my official duties this morning and as my reports have not been returned I am pretty sure all will be all right. . . . I did not get paid in Washington, the Paymaster being absent. I came from Washington with Colonel Danks of the 63rd Pa. Regt. His orderly met him at the station with his horse. The Colonel very kindly dismounted the orderly, thereby saving me a tramp through two miles of mud. Mud, however, is no name for the villainous compound in this vicinity—the entire country being nothing more or less than a*

vast mortar bed. My Regt. is in the 2nd Brigade, 3rd Division, 2nd Corps. The Brigade contains nine old Kearny Regts. So you may know it is a good one. It is commanded by Genl. Alexander Hays, recently in command of the 3rd Div., 2nd Corps.[4]

In a reorganization of the army, the 105th Regiment found itself in the 2nd Brigade, along with the 57th and 63rd Pennsylvania, the 4th and 17th Maine, the 3rd and 5th Michigan, the 93rd New York, and the 1st U.S. Sharpshooters. This group was more diversified than the old all-Pennsylvania brigade. The commander of the 3rd Division was General Birney, and of the 2nd Corps one of the most dynamic Union leaders, Major General Winfield Scott Hancock.

The quiet was about to be broken. Congress having created the rank of lieutenant general, Lincoln nominated Grant for this rank and on March 12 gently pushed Halleck aside in an order that gave the new lieutenant general "command of the armies of the United States." He planned a grand offensive on several fronts simultaneously: against Lee in Virginia, against Richmond, against General Johnston in Georgia. He introduced a new kind of objective: instead of taking places, like Richmond, he proposed to mop up enemy armies. This plan was supported by the reasoning that once they were disposed of, resistance must collapse. Grant made his headquarters at Culpeper Court House, where he was the real director of events, although Meade technically retained command of the Army of the Potomac.

This force to be thrown against Lee began crossing the Rapidan by several fords on May 4. Almost immediately it found itself in the tangled wilderness of scrub oaks, underbrush, and fallen timber and fighting a confusing, uncoordinated series of fierce battles with the Army of Northern Virginia. Lee, though outnumbered, handled his troops so skillfully that Grant gained no ground while losing about 18,000 men in three days. On May 7, Major Watson found time for a few words:

> *So far I have escaped safely. We have experienced one of the hardest fights the last two days we have ever had. Our troops have behaved splendidly—especially our Division. Our Brigade is all cut to pieces. Lost our Brigade Commander, Genl. Hays, and 1700 men. Col. Craig and Lieut. Col. Greenewalt are both seriously wounded. The latter, I fear, will die. Capt. Hamilton and Capt. Clyde were both killed. In fact, the Regt. is all used up. The fight is not decided yet. Still we all feel sanguine of victory. . . . I will write again at the first opportunity.*[5]

On May 6, Hancock's 2nd Corps, in the forefront of an attack ordered by Meade, had engaged in deadly hand-to-hand combat. Later, vicious assaults upon Hancock's forces forced retirement; in the day's melee, the 2nd Corps, 2nd Brigade, and 105th Pennsylvania lost heavily. Failing to dent the enemy front, Grant sidled off in a southeasterly direction. This move pleased veterans of the Army of the Potomac; they were cheered by a general who, unlike other commanders of the army, did not retreat after being checked. Lee kept pace with Grant and, beginning on May 8 at Spotsylvania, the two armies clashed again during twelve days of fights that resulted in another 18,000 Union casualties. On May 12, Lieutenant A. H. Mitchell, of the 105th Pennsylvania, distinguished himself and brought honor to the regiment by capturing an enemy battle flag.

In the midst of these battles, Major Watson, in urgent need of supplies, addressed on May 19 a formal, but forceful, letter to some superior identified only as "Doctor":

> *I have in charge 275 wounded, including 50 amputations and resections and have neither food, clothing, nor supplies of any kind, the men have been living on hard bread and water for three days, the Coffee was expended on Sunday 12th, the sugar on the 13th, and I feel satisfied that many have already died from want of proper sustenance. I applied to Dr. Dalton for relief through the Chaplain of the 93rd N.Y. The Dr. replied that he could send none without permission of Genl. Grant, our last cracker was issued this morning and if relief is not afforded the men will die of sheer starvation. I applied to the Confederates, they replied that nothing prevented us from receiving supplies from our own lines.*[6]

Whether or not Major Watson received the needed supplies is not evident. It is easy to imagine his indignation over this breakdown at a critical time. But since he was determined and resourceful, we may surmise and hope that he cut through the red tape swathing a hidebound superior who refused to act in an emergency without the approval of General Grant.

Stalemated at Spotsylvania, Grant again slid off to the southeast, Lee followed, and at North Anna River another five days of conflict occurred, sharp though less costly this time. Once again the armies moved as before to initiate at Cold Harbor on June 1 more than ten days of assaults and counterassaults that further depleted the Army of the Potomac by more than 11,000. In this campaign of about five weeks, Union losses were frightful: more than 7,000 killed, more than 35,000 wounded. Northern states, with a reserve of manpower, supplied replacements, but the carnage shocked Union supporters; even the usually imperturbable Grant was shaken.

Major Watson, separated from his regiment since the second day of the battles of the Wilderness, remained on hospital duty there for more than three weeks. Finally getting away, he wrote from White House, Virginia, on June 1:

> *I was twenty three days in the Wilderness. The rebels refused to permit us to be taken out under flag of truce. So last Saturday 3 Regts. Cavalry and one of Infantry with 36 Ambulances were sent after me. The rebel pickets were driven in and we were triumphantly taken to Fredericksburg where we embarked on a transport and under the protection of a Gun boat sailed for Port Royal. Upon arriving there we found it just being evacuated. The wounded went on to Washington and I and Dr. O'Farrell, the only Medical Officer that still remained with me (for we were the last two of our army out of the wilderness) took a steamer for the White House—where we arrived yesterday. We were 3 days on the way although the distance is but 250 miles. I have roughed it a good deal since I have been in the service but the last 3 weeks' experience exceeds any thing I have ever before encountered. I intend joining my Regt. as soon as possible. So far I have been unable to find where our Corps is. A Corps Hospital is being formed here—but I will not stay as I am very anxious to get to my Regt. in order to hear from home.*

I have not heard a thing from the Regt. since the 6th of May—neither do I know any thing of Army movements. Some of Genl. Butler's troops who are here say Butler was badly whipped at Drewry's Bluff. We sailed from Port Royal to mouth of the Rappahannock which empties into the Chesapeake Bay, and down the Bay to York River, up York to the Pamunkey and up the Pamunkey to White House. It would have been a very pleasant sail if we had had any thing to eat. But I was without food for 36 hours.[7]

General Butler was indeed badly whipped at Drewry's Bluff. Assigned the task of advancing on Richmond, he bungled it and, after a disastrous repulse, found himself bottled up by General Pierre Beauregard on a narrow strip of land between the James and Appomattox Rivers. Of all the inept Union generals given command for political reasons, Benjamin F. Butler was one of the worst. By the middle of June the Army of the Potomac had crossed the James at Wilcox's Landing and had come to a halt before Petersburg, where it settled down for a long siege. Both sides built interlocking series of forts and engaged in frequent sorties, but the town did not fall for more than nine months.

*A*PPARENTLY MAJOR WATSON did not rejoin his regiment. He spent the summer and most of the autumn on duty at 3rd Division Hospital. From there he wrote on August 19:

I am very busy here, over 700 sick and wounded in my Division. I have only 3 Medical Officers and am compelled to attend a section containing over 150 patients myself. . . . There are over

2000 patients in this Corps. Thinking a trip would do me good and afford me some recreation I was, at my own request, detailed in charge of the Steamer City of Albany and went up the James River to Deep Bottom for the wounded of the 2nd Corps. I was gone two days and never had more laborious work in my life. Henry did not like the idea of my going up—and said, "Doctor, you are too venturesome"—but Henry's pluck, as you well know, is none of the best. I brought down 450, including 150 Cavalry. . . . I had the sad duty of bringing down the remains of Col. Craig. He was shot in the head and died in 14 hours. Never spoke after he was hit. He had command of the Brigade and his loss will be deeply felt. He was one of the finest Officers in the Division. . . . My old friend, Capt. Barr, I fear, is mortally wounded—the ball passing in at the ear and going out at the back of the neck. We have lost in this Campaign every field Officer, 3 of our most efficient Captains, and several Lieutenants. Almost every Officer in the Regt. has been wounded. When I return to it I fear it will not seem like home. If it is filled up Capt. Conser will have command. . . . He was shot several months since in the thigh. The ball is still in but troubles very little. The last move, like all former ones before Petersburg has resulted in a miserable failure. Our loss in the last action in the 2nd and 10 Corps will exceed 3000 and nothing accomplished. Go where we will and Genl. Lee presents a bold front. It is fight, fight and constant defeat. It is almost impossible, owing to our many and disastrous defeats, to get our men to charge the rebel works. They have been charged till they themselves say it is "played out." I have every confidence in Grant's ultimate success—but the army has received so many repeated repulses that the soldiers are dispirited. Grant, I fear, will have to wait for reinforcements—his veterans will not charge as they did at the beginning of the Campaign and besides this they require rest—especially the 2nd Corps.[8]

The sniping and almost daily fights before and around Petersburg took their toll. From the middle of June to the first of October, Union losses were about 3,000 killed, almost 20,000 wounded. Major Watson had no respite from hospital duty. On September 4 he wrote to his youngest sister, Marie:

I can not let my birth day pass without sending a kiss to you, Pa, the Girls, and baby. I am getting old, my dear Puddie and if I did not have my birth day to remind me of it my gray hairs would—for without joking I am getting fearfully frosty. It is very late at night, nearly 1 o'clock, so you will have to indulge me in a very brief letter—and besides this I am very tired, having just returned from the front. I started this afternoon between 2 and 3 o'clock to visit my Regt. distant 15 miles and found it in the rifle pits on the right of the 5th Corps. My friend, Capt. Patton, was Brigade Officer of the day and just about visiting the picket line. I accompanied him. At some points the lines are only 150 yards apart and in one place but 50. I was close enough to them to see their eyes and distinguish the color of their hair—I mean the Rebs. The pickets in front of our Corps have ceased firing by mutual consent—although farther to the right in front of the 10th and 18th Corps the firing is constant. . . . Some of our forts are not over 4 hundred yards from the rebel works. Our soldiers and the rebels have bomb proofs into which they crawl whenever the Artillery firing begins. In returning I got lost and ran into the pickets of the 10th Corps and did not discover my mistake until I heard the pickets firing. It was very dark and balls flying all around did not make it the most pleasant place in the world. It is needless to say that I beat a very hasty retreat. I send you, my dear Pud, a rough sketch of my Quarters taken by a little drummer Boy. They are composed of 3 Hospital tents. You observe a flag in front—it is a yellow flag with a red diamond in the centre—our Division badge. You will also observe a guard. I have one day and night for my Hospital is conducted in accordance with strict military discipline. The front tent is occupied by the clerk and orderlies. The middle is my private office, and the other my sleeping apartment. The tents are all nicely floored—so you see I am fixed very comfortably. I have three orderlies—Bob, Dick and "Dixie." Bob is 16 years old and a real Yankee boy from New Hampshire. Dick is 14 and from New York—and Dixie is a drummer boy from my Regt. and the same age as Dick. They are all fine boys and have plenty to do as I have a great many orders to issue and messages to send. Dixie says he will never leave me. He is very intelligent and very handsome and if I can get him out of the Service when my time expires I will bring him home with me.[9]

On this birthday the major was only twenty-seven, but his feeling of hoary age was surely genuine. Two years of bitter conflict, of hard marches, suffering, and bloodshed had been harrowing enough to frost anybody's hair. Dispirited troops before Petersburg reflected the sagging morale of the whole North. In the summer of 1864 the Union cause was as close to failure as it had ever been. An apparently interminable war, exacting a terrible price in lives and treasure, caused widespread weariness and despair. This gloom, abetted by copperheads and fifth-column defeatists, increased the popularity of McClellan, who was running on a peace platform as Democratic candidate for president. Lincoln was so dubious of re-election that he prepared a statement in which he offered to cooperate with the next president-elect in a last-ditch effort to save the Union.

The young orderlies the major mentions typify the youthfulness of this army. All armies are composed of young men, but those of the Civil War were younger than most. Enrolled in Union ranks during the four years were 800,000 boys not older than seventeen; of these, 100,000 were no more than fifteen, and among them were 300 thirteen-year-olds. The drummer boy was a hardy creature—he had to be—celebrated in homespun prose and verse and in one popular postwar play, *The Drummer Boy of the Shenandoah.*

AROUND PETERSBURG the armies continued to cut and thrust. On September 30 the major wrote:

> *The entire Army is now on the move and every one is sanguine respecting the capture of Richmond. Genl. Butler, with the 10th and 18th Army Corps, is between Fort Darling and Richmond while Genl. Meade holds the line in front of Petersburg with a portion of his force and has massed the remainder on the left. Genl. Butler is reported to have driven the enemy, captured 20 pieces of Artillery and advanced to within 5 or 6 miles of Richmond. Richmond threatened, the enemy will be compelled to concentrate on the right—and this will give Genl. Meade a*

chance to make a successful dash on Petersburg. So we are sure of Petersburg or Richmond and probably of both. Genl. Grant is determined to capture one or both Cities or "bust the machine." This evening we have heard very heavy firing on the left—but have heard nothing of the result. . . . The 63rd Pa. Vols. is now consolidated with our Regt. We number over 700 men—nearly enough to muster the full complement of field Officers. Therefore I am afraid my chance of getting out of the Service is rather slim. . . . I will tender my resignation at the conclusion of the fall Campaign—but I fear it will be disapproved. I have received my pay up to the 1st October, two months. While the pay is diminishing my expenses are increasing. I have never been so economical in all my life. Have positively for the last five months not spent one cent except for tobacco and rations. Every thing is enormously dear. I could not live half so well or cheap if I did not sponge pretty freely on the Sanitary and Hospital. . . . You will certainly hear good news soon. Grant will whip Lee, Old Abe will be reelected and the Union preserved. I held a vote in my Division and old Abe received 86 majority.[10]

The expected good news from this front was not forthcoming. Butler's offensive at New Market Heights, about ten miles southeast of Richmond, failed, naturally, with a loss of 2,500 men. Meade, at Poplar Springs Church, near Petersburg, got nowhere while losing 2,800. To subdue either place, Grant might be forced, as the major said, to bust the machine. But while stalemate frustrated the Army of the Potomac, better news came from other sectors. Admiral David Farragut closed the port of Mobile; Sherman captured Atlanta; Sheridan's cavalry swept the enemy from the Shenandoah valley. These successes gave a much-needed boost to Union fortunes and practically assured Lincoln's reelection. The straw vote in Major Watson's division was almost accurate. Voting late in October, the 105th Pennsylvania cast 136 ballots for Lincoln, 73 for McClellan.

The major, evidently borne down by war fatigue, seemed eager to leave the army. On October 24 he wrote:

I have been anxiously expecting a letter for some days in order to learn the result of our district elections. . . . My proxy came too late to send home. I only received it the morning of election. I voted here, however. . . . I received your letter stating Genl. Russell would assist me in getting my resignation accepted. The trouble is my papers will not go to the Surgeon Genl. or the Secretary of War but to Army Head Quarters—and will have to be transmitted through Brigade, Division and Corps Head Quarters—at all of which places I am positive they will be disapproved. Surgeons are getting mighty scarce in the Army and all that are good for any thing will be held till the expiration of their time. If I can get home, however, I can forward my resignation direct to the Secretary of War through the Adjutant General's office and then the Genl.'s influence can easily be brought to bear. The Army, I think, is just on the eve of an important movement—which will render it almost impossible to get a leave of absence just now without showing some urgent necessity. If you will write me that my presence is absolutely required at home . . . I very probably can get out [of] the Service. I am very busy now preparing for winter. We are still in tents and, having very few stoves, are compelled to build chimneys. The grounds for our new Hospitals have been selected and the construction of the Barracks will begin this week. I have built myself a splendid house. It is pronounced by all who have seen it to be the best Quarters in the Army. . . . Please have McMullin to make me a pair of boots as soon as possible and forward them by mail. He still owes me a pair. I wish fine boots—but want them plenty large.[11]

Action ensued, costly but indecisive, at Boydton Plank Road and Hatcher's Run, as the major reported on October 29:

I am very busy now, having over one thousand patients in my Hospital. The 2nd Corps has had a very hard fight and from all I can ascertain fared rather badly. Our Regt. was terribly used up—losing 140 guns and their colors. The Boys feel very badly about the loss of the colors. It is the first time they have ever lost their colors although engaged in over 30 battles. Captain Conser, acting Colonel, and Captain Patton, acting Major, were killed. They were the last of the original Officers. . . . Our Regt. was armed with Spencer Rifles, seven shooters. The whole Regt. was captured at one time and only escaped in consequence of night supervening. I don't know why it is but some fearful fatality has pursued all our Senior Officers in this Campaign. We have lost our Col., Major, Lieut. Col., five Senior Captains and a proportionable amount Lieuts. and privates. It has been a splendid Regt.—but I fear its days of glorious deeds have passed. I have performed some ten or twelve Capital Operations to day besides selecting patients for duty and Genl. Hospital. This is not all. I have made out sixteen certificates for wounded Officers and about 30 furloughs for Michigan soldiers in order that they may go home and vote. Consequently I am very tired and you must excuse this letter.[12]

The 105th lost its colors on October 27 in a fight on the Boydton Plank Road. Soldiers felt such a loss more deeply than the capture of guns or prisoners. Still, the regiment, remembering Lieutenant Mitchell's exploit at Spotsylvania, might pride itself on being one of twenty-four Federal units that had captured enemy battle flags.

The Spencer carbine was the latest thing in weapons. A .54 caliber repeater, it was a breach-loader that eliminated the awkward ramrod of muzzle-loaders. The clip was generally eight instead of seven, and cartridge cases were brass. Though of much stronger firepower than old-fashioned arms, it seems not to have materially aided Union troops around Petersburg. The Confederates captured some Spencers, but they could never find brass enough to manufacture cartridge cases.

On October 30, the major wrote a more explicit account of the action involving the 2nd Corps:

I am very busy at present. My Hospital is overcrowded—so full indeed that I was compelled to send some fifty or sixty of my wounded to the 1st Division Hospital. Yesterday and today I have had a great deal of operating. I am pretty well through now. There was such confusion at the front that many requiring operations were sent here untouched. The 2nd Corps had an other very desperate fight in which my Regt. suffered severely. The Regt. . . . repulsed the enemy handsomely the first charge. The Regt. was on the extreme left of the line connecting with the Cavalry—the enemy advanced in overwhelming force and attacked the front, flank and rear, compelling the Regt. to give way. It is reported we lost our colors—this I am inclined to doubt for it is considered very disgraceful for a Regt. to come from a battle field without

*their colors—and I can't think it possible that our Regt., ac-
knowledged by all one of the best in the Army, to have been so
very unfortunate. . . . The papers state the 2nd and 5th Corps
merely went on a reconnaissance and, succeeding in developing
the strength of the enemy, retired to their old positions. To tell the
truth, Pa, this is not so—for we advanced with the intention
and almost certainty of turning the enemy's right flank, capturing the south side railroad, Petersburg and probably Richmond,
in all of which we failed. This of course will not be published—
nevertheless it is true. I must now conclude as I have just received orders to make out with the least possible delay furloughs
for all Connecticut, Rhode Island, New Hampshire and Mass.
troops in my Hospital—in order, I presume, that they may be
present for the Election. This will employ me all night.*[13]

The politics of the Army of the Potomac being predominantly Republican, Lincoln ordered leaves for soldiers
who wanted to go home to vote; whole regiments were
sent off. Major Watson returned to this theme on November 6, and also clarified his views on resigning from
the army:

*I have furloughed over 100 men in order that they may go home
and vote. This morning I sent 140 patients to Genl. Hospital
and returned some 150 to duty. So I will not have so much to do
now. I asked Dr. Dalton this morning if he would approve a
leave of absence for fifteen days for me. He said he would—but
remarked that he thought it useless for me to apply as my application would in all probability be disapproved at Army Head
Quarters. . . . I should like very much to resign in order to assist
Pa but on no other account—for to tell the truth, Em, I don't
like the idea of leaving the Service till the expiration of my time.*

I have been treated very well this summer—having had a very important position during the whole Campaign. The 1st and 2nd Divs. of our Corps have had five or six different Surgeons in charge since I have been here. I have been the only one permanently retained. How long it will last I can't say—probably as long as the Hospital is continued.[14]

Six days later he was relieved from hospital duty and ordered to rejoin his regiment "in consequence," he said, "of the great scarcity of Medical Officers in the front. I have been here a long time on duty and have been relieved because they imagine I have had a soft thing for nearly six months. I will report in person to the Commanding Officer of my Regt. today."[15]

THE YEAR ENDED without positive result at Petersburg, but Union hopes had taken a turn for the better. Lincoln had been reelected, though McClellan polled 45 percent of the popular vote. At Nashville, General Thomas had shattered the army of General J. B. Hood; Sherman, having marched across Georgia, had taken Savannah. The Army of the Potomac, since marching into the Wilderness almost eight months before, had lost so many men by death and wounds that it was no longer the same army it had been in May. In all those weeks of strife it had not once gained a clear-cut victory over the Army of Northern Virginia. Yet these Union troops had performed a valuable service by keeping Lee pinned down, preventing him from exploiting his favorite and dangerous tactic of maneuver, and also by depleting the gray lines of manpower that the Confederacy could not replace. Mean-

while the war was being won elsewhere. Though em-
battled soldiers probably did not sense it, the end was
not far away.

1865

*T*HE ARRIVAL OF A NEW YEAR did not resolve the impasse at Petersburg. For two months, while the Army of the Potomac remained in winter quarters, no major action occurred. Major Watson got a leave, which must have been an agreeable surprise, but by the end of January he had returned to camp. On the twenty-ninth he wrote:

> *In consequence of being ice bound in Baltimore I did not rejoin my Regt. till last Friday. I arrived in Baltimore on Sunday morning and was detained there until Wednesday afternoon.... Nothing was said of my prolonged absence—and I am now on duty as if I had never been absent. The weather is bitterly cold. In fact I have suffered more from the severity of the weather since my return than while home. Capt. Miller, commanding my Regt., has been made Major and is now absent on leave when he expects to be appointed Lieut. Col. I called on Doct. Evarts this morning (he is Surgeon in Chief of our Div.) and told him I intended resigning and explained the reasons. He said he would approve my papers and endorse them strongly. I will see*

tomorrow whether the Capt. Commanding the Regt. will approve them and if so will forward them immediately. If Capt. Miller were here I think he would. Genl. Peirce is absent and Genl. West is commanding our Brigade. I am very sorry for this as I feel sure Genl. Peirce would approve my papers. Nevertheless I will try and have strong hopes of success. . . . I hope by this time the Girls have received their skates and are enjoying the ice.[1]

Within two weeks he formally submitted his resignation, then waited while his papers slowly traveled up the chain of command. On February 25 he wrote:

Ten days have passed since my papers went up and still they have not been returned. I can't conceive why they are so long delayed. A clerk from our Regt. and on duty at Corps told me last night that my papers had been disapproved at Corps Head Quarters. I don't know how much reliance is to be placed on his report. . . . The war news is gloriously encouraging. In addition to the fall of Charleston a circular has just been issued from Army Head Quarters informing the troops of the evacuation of Wilmington and the probable evacuation of Petersburg. We are under marching orders now and as there was very heavy Artillery firing all day in front of Petersburg the inference is that Genl. Grant is watching Lee very closely and is prepared to take immediate advantage of any movement Lee may hazard. My horse was injured while I was absent and has not been fit for use since my return. He is hurt in the right shoulder and over the Kidneys and can scarcely move—so if I remain in the service I will have to purchase an other one. . . . You will remember I told you when home that I would never again take a position away from my Regt. I will explain in a few words. Genl. West was in command of our Brig. and being personally unacquainted with the Genl. I accepted the position in order that, being on his Staff, I might, without violation of military orders and etiquette, approach and consult him in person respecting my resignation. If the latter is disapproved I will ask to be returned to my Regt. immediately. Brigade Head Quarters are but a few steps from my Regt. and the Genl. has given me permission to remain with it till I hear from my papers. I go there once a day to transact business—and there is mighty little of that to do, I assure you.[2]

The war news was indeed cheering. Fort Fisher had been captured in late January with the aid of Admiral Porter's North Atlantic squadron—after fumbling General Butler had botched the job of taking it three weeks earlier. Wilmington, last port open to the Confederacy, had fallen in late February. Sherman was marching through the Carolinas. Federal cavalry ranged more freely than heretofore. The major's papers, lost somewhere in the mill of army communications, never showed up, but when he was informed that his resignation had been disapproved, he accepted the verdict philosophically.

In his next letter, on March 18, he momentarily turned aside from war to consider a macabre combination of local events:

Our Div. was paraded this morning for the purpose of witnessing the death of a deserter. He was shot in compliance with orders from the Genl. Court Martial of our Div. by the Provost Guard. Was to have been shot yesterday—but the sentence was deferred on account of the races. Yesterday, being St. Patrick's day, was a grand holiday in the army especially with the Irish element. There were some fine horse races. Every portion of the

*army from the James River to Hatcher's Run was largely repre-
sented. A citizen from Baltimore brought down two private race
horses, a Bay and Gray. The former was beaten but the latter
won a race. The betting was very heavy. At 4 o'clock in the
evening there was a race in the 5th Corps between "Yankee Dan,"
a celebrated running horse belonging to a Captain in the 2nd
Corps, and a gray Stallion from the 5th Corps who had never
been beaten. "Yankee Dan" was victorious and the 5th Corps of
course lost a pile of Green backs. We have been under marching
orders for several days—all surplus baggage and tents have been
turned in and sent to the rear and we are in such shape as to
enable us to move off at a moment's notice. . . . Genl. Grant is
watching Lee so closely that it will be a very difficult matter for
the latter Gentleman to give Grant the slip.*[3]

*E*VENTS MOVED RAPIDLY in the final climactic three
weeks. In late March, General John Brown Gordon's
spirited but futile assault on the right of the Union line
was the last aggressive action of the Army of Northern
Virginia. On April 2 a massive Union attack broke through
the outer lines of Petersburg and forced the defenders to
withdraw to inner works. The long siege was over. Lee
evacuated the town and started his army toward Lynch-
burg, but he did not reach it. The end came at Appomattox, where the Army of Northern Virginia surrendered
on April 9. Five days later Lincoln was assassinated. Major
Watson's next letter, on April 18, briefly touched upon
these momentous happenings:

*Our felicitations over the defeat and capture of the Army of
Northern Virginia were suddenly hushed by the sad intelligence*

of Mr. Lincoln's assassination. Every officer and soldier whom I have conversed with say they would sooner have lost any other public man in the country, not excepting Grant and Sherman. Mr. Lincoln had the respect and love of every true soldier and loyal man in the country. No particulars of his death have been received. The fact was merely communicated by telegraph. Yesterday seven rebels were hung in the vicinity of the Station. They were caught tearing up the Railroad. I understand they were paroled prisoners and of course were in honor bound not to commit any act of hostility against the Government till exchanged. They violated their parole and were justly and summarily dealt with. There is no truth or honor in a Rebel. This I know from experience. My horse, as I informed you in a prior letter, was used up and I was compelled to purchase an other. I could not obtain a good one and therefore bought one for seventy five dollars. The Horse gave out on the march and I abandoned him. When the rebels surrendered Genl. Grant permitted the Officers to retain their private Horses and baggage and many of their Officers, anxious to get home, speedily sold their horses to our officers. I purchased a splendid blind bay from Capt. Pace, Asst. Adjut. Genl. to Genl. Gordon. He told me he brought the horse from Georgia and had used him 2 years. I gave him one hundred and fifty dollars for him. After having him several days and having him well groomed I discovered a U.S. on him. He certainly had been captured from us and this Officer certainly knew it. Still he pledged his honor he was a private Horse. Capt. Pace was Asst. Adjut. Genl. and Inspector Genl. of the 2nd Corps, Army of Northern Virginia. When a man in his position wilfully pledges his honor to a lie you may be certain there is but little truth in the rank and file. I can retain the Horse of course but whether I will be permitted to bring him home is an other *question. If I am not, my $150 are gone up. . . . I captured on the march one of the finest Amputating case of instruments I have ever seen. It was made by Kolbe and certainly did not cost less than 60 or 75 dollars. This I will bring home with me. There were any amount of fine double barrel guns captured. Our Regt. lost but 3 killed and 24 wounded during the whole campaign. Our Corps pressed the rear of the Rebels from Petersburg to where they surrendered and consequently did not have the same opportunity of flanking and making large captures as some of the other Corps. Still the 2 Corps captured 35 pieces of Artillery—400 wagons—5000 prisoners and 15 battle flags. Our Regt. in one charge captured 199 men and 14 Officers. Good for the 105th, was it not?[4]*

*F*OR THE NEXT THREE WEEKS the 2nd Corps remained near Burkesville Station, where camp life, undisturbed by campaigns in the offing, became relaxed. "Our time," wrote Major Watson on April 27,

is mainly passed in discussing the many idle and improbable camp rumors regarding the speedy suspension of hostilities, the movement and location of the different Corps, the disbandonment of the Army, and the surrender of Johnston. One moment it is reported Johnston has surrendered, the next that he and his army with Jeff Davis have escaped to Texas where they intend making a stand—and that the 2 Corps have orders to go there without delay. An hour after, some one just from Corps Head Quarters reports that the 2 Corps has been ordered to join Genl. Hancock. In fact there are so many rumors that you can't believe a word you hear—consequently I can't form the least idea what disposition will be made of this army or how soon it will be disbanded and we permitted to return to our homes. All agree, however, that the Army of the Potomac has done its last fighting. There is not one Officer or man in this Army who is not indignant at the terms accorded by Sherman to Johnston—for there was not a man here who would not willingly have marched to his assistance in order to secure the unconditional surrender of Johnston. This Army was greatly dissatisfied at the terms granted Lee and you may know well that after his surrender and the assassination of the President they would not willingly sanction terms which awarded pardon and protection of life and property to the vilest rebel, an acknowledgment of State's rights, permission to retain their arms, and finally terms which entirely ignore the President's emancipation proclamation. Sherman is a gallant soldier and has always out generalled his opponents—but this attempt to assume civil and political authority not vested in him is exceedingly unfortunate and I fear will greatly impair his usefulness and popularity. The rebel confederacy is gone up and rebel arrogance and treasonable language and action, both North and South, must be suppressed by severe and summary punishment. I have no confidence in rebel honor, integrity or loyalty. No, not a bit.[5]

$\mathcal{S}$HERMAN'S FIRST TERMS TO JOHNSTON, including general amnesty for his army, had been too generous for Washington. Stanton promptly rejected them, and they were revised to essentially the same terms Grant gave to Lee at Appomattox. Whether Lincoln himself would have accepted the original terms is one of those tantalizing "ifs" of history. Sherman, a compassionate man when the fighting was over, was probably trying to carry out

Lincoln's injunction to his top commanders: "Let 'em up easy." Major Watson's indignation indicates the strong tides of emotion that engulfed partisans in this war, especially after the assassination of the president. Yet in the light of the bitter aftermath, when punitive measures and harsh reconstruction were engineered by vindictive politicians, Sherman's generosity seems the wiser course. He may have lost popularity, but only temporarily, for he was later asked to be the Republican candidate for president. He firmly replied that he would not run, nor would he serve if elected.

Major Watson returned to the surrender theme in a letter the next day, April 28:

> *A telegram has just been received officially announcing the surrender of Genl. Johnston on the same terms as Genl. Lee. The intelligence was received by the army with great satisfaction but with little enthusiasm as Johnston's surrender was daily expected. I had sincerely hoped Johnston would violate the Armistice by trying to slip off and in this way afford Sherman a chance to retrieve his error before the arrival of Genl. Grant. But in this I have been disappointed for the Secretary of War dispatches that Grant arrived in Raleigh on Monday, the 24th, and communicated to Sherman the disapproval of his course by the President and his Cabinet and also notified Johnston of the fact and that hostilities would be instantly resumed. On the announcement of Grant's determination, Johnston immediately surrendered. Sherman could easily have enforced the same terms but unfortunately did not push his advantage and has therefore greatly dimmed the bright lustre of his fair military character. I feel sorry for Genl. Sherman, very sorry indeed, for he*

was my Hero and favorite General. I trust, however, his valuable services to the country will more than compensate for this one error and that he will be continued in his command and afforded an opportunity to retrieve himself. Sherman's case demonstrates that military fame at best is but a fickle Goddess and that one blunder will often ruin the well earned reputation of years. The military power of the so called Southern Confederacy is annihilated, the fighting over and as soon as order is restored and Civil law established in the rebellious States the greater part of the army will be disbanded. I cannot tell you, my Dear Sister, how thankful I am for the disapproval of my resignation. I would not have been a Civilian during the recent successes achieved by the Army of the Potomac for untold gold. I can, if I desire, get a leave of absence for 20 days but this luxury I am too poor to afford. I have been living on credit ever since I purchased my last horse. . . . I think it would be very unjust for Uncle Sam to take the horse from me. He was captured by the enemy and in my opinion belonged to the enemy and not to Uncle Sam. . . . I have made a few female acquaintances in this vicinity. A family sent to Genl. Peirce for a Physician and I, being Brigade Surgeon and desiring exercise, volunteered my very eminent services. In one House there are five young Ladies, in an other four—all well educated and mighty fine Girls, I can tell you. I have visited them frequently since and find it a very pleasant and agreeable way of spending my unoccupied time. . . . It is night and the troops have suddenly begun to cheer and fire off guns and seem to be in a mad state of excitement. I must go out and ascertain the cause. Well, I have been out and am informed that Jeff Davis is captured. I find the news is not official, merely a Camp rumor and give it to you as such. I sincerely trust the report is correct as I should be very sorry to see the old Scamp escape with a half million dollars in Specie. . . . I wrote Pa yesterday and Marie several days before, asking her to send me some stamps and a few silk pocket Handkerchiefs. . . . Official information has been received that Booth has been shot. Thank God, the villain has not been permitted to escape.[6]

Johnston surrendered to Sherman in North Carolina on April 26. The report of the capture of Jefferson Davis was premature. When the fall of Petersburg and Richmond seemed imminent, he had fled south with the funds that remained in the treasury, apparently intending either to continue a provisional government or to join whatever Confederate force remained in the field. In Georgia he was overtaken and captured by a detachment of the 4th Michigan cavalry on May 10.

Major Watson's lack of money and stamps repeats an old refrain. Evidently the Union supply system remained, in some ways, unsystematic to the end. After almost a month near Burkesville Station, the Army of the Potomac prepared to move, though not into battle this time. "The Army will start tomorrow," wrote the major on May 2,

> *for Alexandria where in all probability we will be mustered out by the 1st of June. The route of the 2 Corps, I understand, is first to Manchester, situated on the opposite side of the James from Richmond, then to Belle Plain via Fredericksburg where we will draw supplies and then march to Alexandria via Stafford Court House and Dumfries. The distance is some 220 miles and as we march the whole way it will require some 14 or 18 days to accomplish the journey. It will, after our arrival, require several weeks to make out the Muster rolls and papers—so prob-*

ably I may not get home till the middle of June. I could, I suppose, resign but do not wish to do so as the war is virtually over. There is an act of Congress appropriating 3 months' pay proper to every Officer remaining in Service till the expiration of the war. My pay proper is 80 dollars a month—so if I remain I will get 240 dollars. There is no doubt in the world that all the Army will be almost immediately disbanded excepting the Regulars . . . and the Cavalry. We shall probably get no mails when we are on the march—so do not be uneasy about me should you not hear from me for some little time. I will write, however, whenever I get the chance. . . . From all I can understand, most of my letters miscarry. This I can't account for as I write very frequently.[7]

A march of 220 miles was no great chore for veteran soldiers heading toward home. They must have stepped out briskly, for they made the distance to Alexandria in about twelve days. From there the major wrote on May 15:

We are located some four miles from Alexandria and as our trains are just arrived all hands are busy washing, changing clothes and fixing up quarters. I have not had a change of clothing for more than two weeks and am, to say the least, particularly filthy. Our long and fatiguing march is now over . . . and I am anxiously awaiting the time when I shall be mustered out of Uncle Sam's Service. I don't know when our Regt. or in fact any of the troops will be mustered out—but as the war is over it certainly will be a very short time. . . . You Girls must not expect too much from me when I return to Civil life for you know I was a pretty rough customer before leaving home and military life, I assure you, has not improved me. I must now conclude as I am sitting in a pine thicket covered with dirt and dust and if I do not go to work will have to sleep in the open air again

*tonight for you must know that during this entire march I have
not had a tent to sleep in. I received Marie's letter containing
the stamps and Handkerchief for which she has my warmest
thanks.*[8]

It is difficult to imagine the major as truly a "rough customer," yet his forthright independence might have made
him seem so in a decorous civilian society. He was undoubtedly right in warning his sisters that military life
was hardly a school for genteel manners. The war was
not quite over, for the Army of the Trans-Mississippi,
commanded by General E. Kirby Smith, remained in the
field. The last to quit, he surrendered on May 26. On the
same day all Confederate prisoners were paroled, and
the war came to a definite end. Major Watson wrote his
last letter as a soldier from a camp near Washington on
May 21:

*I am quite busy now arranging my papers so as to avoid all
unnecessary delay when I am discharged the service. . . . An
order has been issued from the war department instructing Commanding Generals to have mustered out all men whose term of
service expires prior to the 1st of October. This order, I presume,
includes Officers as well as men. I intend seeing the Division
Mustering Officer tomorrow and if I come under the provisions
of said order will demand my muster out immediately. The Officers and men of my Regt. are opposed to my leaving—but this
I can not help. Our Regt. numbers nearly 1000 men and as
most of them are new recruits and the remaining number veterans the organization will in all probability be retained. It is
impossible at present to say what disposition will be made of
the troops. But after the review I think it will be officially an-*

nounced which Regimental organizations will be retained. . . .
The Review will be a big thing and I shall feel pretty disap-
pointed if Pa does not come down. I have applied for a 24 hours'
pass to Washington in order to try and get some pay and cloth-
ing. I am very hard up for cash and have been living on credit
ever since I bought my horse. . . . You should see my pets—four
young Crows. I have had them several weeks. They are very
tame and growing rapidly.[9]

In the grand review on May 23–24, 150,000 men of the
armies of the Potomac, the Tennessee, and Georgia paraded the streets of Washington. It is to be hoped that
the major got his twenty-four-hour pass, that he got his
pay and perhaps a new uniform in which to be resplen-
dent with his regiment when it marched down Pennsylvania Avenue on the twenty-third—though he just might
have preferred to appear in the worn battle dress of the
veteran campaigner. Then the armies melted away into
civilian life.

The 105th Regiment had seen such hard service
that, when it was mustered out, not a single officer remained of the original command, and but a handful of
men. Major Watson, discharged on May 27, returned to
Bedford, where he practiced medicine for the rest of his
life, and duly joined the G. A. R., though he was not
given to patriotic orations at reunions. Possibly the rigors of war hastened his end, for he did not long survive
the conflict, dying at the early age of forty-one in 1879.
Afterward, the town honored his memory by naming the
militia camp near Bedford Camp Watson.

Notes

1862

1. To William Hartley Watson from Harrisburg, Pennsylvania, September 16, 1862. A popular pastime of the soldier, whether veteran or recruit, was to have his photograph taken and printed on a small card, called *carte de visite,* suitable for mailing home to family and best girl. Some of these photographs look very warlike: full uniform, musket, perhaps a pistol or two, occasionally a knife. Yet belligerence is belied by the young faces that look out at us.

2. To William Hartley Watson from roadside inn near Alexandria, Virginia, September 17, 1862. A Sibley tent was large, circular, and conical, capable of housing a dozen men or more. They slept in a circle, feet toward a fire in the center. Gideon was probably a friend from Bedford.

3. To William Hartley Watson from Washington, D.C., September 18, 1862.

4. To William Hartley Watson from Camp Prescott, Virginia, September 20, 1862. Camp Prescott (Smith) was near Arlington Heights, Virginia. A sutler was a civilian provisioner to an army post.

5. To Emma Watson from Camp Prescott, Virginia, September 24, 1862. Miss Sue, a Bedford friend, was evidently a Southern sympathizer, a not uncommon sort, even in such a predominantly Union state as Pennsylvania.

6. To William Hartley Watson from Camp Prescott, Virginia, September 26, 1862. Wat, a cousin of Major Watson, was a trooper in the 2nd Pennsylvania Cavalry, which at that time was encamped about two miles from the 105th Infantry. Tom Richardson was a Bedford friend. The proclamation that Watson refers to is the Emancipation Proclamation, issued on September 22, five days after the slim Union margin of victory at the Battle of Antietam gave Lincoln the military success needed to make the proclamation psychologically effective.

7. To Ella Watson from Camp Prescott, Virginia, September 27, 1862.

8. To William Hartley Watson from Camp Prescott Smith, Virginia, September 29, 1862.

9. Ibid., October 8, 1862. The name "Surrett" raises the question whether—Major Watson perhaps misspelling the name—she was any connection of the Mary E. Surratt who was one of eight convicted of conspiracy to assassinate Lincoln.

10. Ibid.

11. To Ella Watson from camp near Poolesville, Maryland, October 13, 1862. Poolesville was a short distance north of the Potomac River, about twenty-five miles above Washington; Conrad's Ferry was in the near vicinity.

12. To William Hartley Watson from camp near Poolesville, Maryland, October 13, 1862.

13. Ibid., October 15, 1862. Brigadier General George Stoneman, commanding Kearny's old division, soon moved up to command of the 3rd Army Corps, and in 1863, as a major general, to command of the Cavalry Corps, Army of the Potomac. Brigadier General Hiram G. Berry, brigade commander, later became a major general; he was killed at Chancellorsville in May 1863. Brigadier General David E. Birney, brigade commander, became a major general and led a division in the Fredericksburg campaign of December 1862.

14. To Eliza Watson from camp near Poolesville, Maryland, October 19, 1862.

15. To Ella Watson from camp near Poolesville, Maryland, October 23, 1862. A gum blanket was rain gear, of the same category

as "gum boots," useful for shedding water, but without the warmth of wool.

16. To William Hartley Watson from camp near Poolesville, Maryland, October 26, 1862.

17. Ibid.

18. To William Hartley Watson from camp near Leesburg, Virginia, October 30, 1862. Jack was Major Watson's bird dog back home.

19. Ibid., October 31, 1862. The words of Walt Whitman following this letter are in his letter to Nat and Fred Gray from Washington, March 19, 1863 (*The Uncollected Poetry and Prose of Walt Whitman,* 2:23).

20. To Eliza Watson from camp south of Leesburg, Virginia, November 1, 1862. Officers' wives were not uncommon in camp, particularly when troops settled down in winter quarters; then military life became more leisurely, and for some more domestic. Units near Washington were constantly visited by admiring ladies, including the famous beauty Kate Chase Sprague, of whom Matthew Brady has left us at least one picture, showing her holding court before an officer's tent. As a rule, wives did not accompany the army on marches, though the hospital steward's wife seems to have done so. On a campaign, with hard fighting in prospect, women were left behind; courageous nurses of the Sanitary Commission, however, were generally close to the front.

21. To William Hartley Watson from camp at the Rappahannock River, Virginia, November 9, 1862. This letter is dated October 9, but the contents make it clear that the major, usually careful about dates, this time got them mixed. Captain John C. Conser commanded Company H of the 105th Regiment; Dr. George W. Ewing was Major Watson's first assistant surgeon. Major General Fitz John Porter, commander of the 5th Army Corps, had been with McClellan on the Peninsula and at the Battle of Antietam. Porter's appearance at Middleburg, Virginia, about six weeks after the battle reveals McClellan's sluggishness.

22. Ibid., November 10, 1862.

23. To Emma Watson from camp near Warrenton, Virginia, November 13, 1862. At this time, Major General Joseph Hooker commanded

the 1st Corps, Army of the Potomac; Major General Franz Sigel, the 11th Corps; and Major General E. V. Sumner, the 2nd Corps.

24. To William Hartley Watson from camp near Warrenton, Virginia, November 14, 1862.

25. To Eliza Watson from camp near Fredericksburg, Virginia, November 24, 1862. Barclay was a Bedford friend.

26. To William Hartley Watson from camp near Fredericksburg, Virginia, November 26, 1862. Dr. Adam Wenger was Major Watson's second assistant surgeon.

27. To Ella Watson from camp near Fredericksburg, Virginia, November 28, 1862. The crude stove that Major Watson describes was typical of soldiers' cleverness at making themselves comfortable. When an army settled down for a while in camp, ingenious improvements appeared: board sides for tents, plank floors, barrel chimneys, even entire log houses with brick fireplaces.

28. To William Hartley Watson from camp near Fredericksburg, Virginia, December 1, 1862.

29. To Emma Watson from camp near Fredericksburg, Virginia, December 2, 1862.

30. To Marie Watson from camp near Fredericksburg, Virginia, December 4, 1862.

31. To William Hartley Watson from camp near Fredericksburg, Virginia, December 10, 1862.

32. To William Hartley Watson from the battlefield near Fredericksburg, Virginia, December 15, 1862. Brigadier General George D. Bayard was killed on December 14. Captain James Hamilton commanded Company I of the 105th Regiment. Major General William Buel Franklin commanded the Left Grand Division at Fredericksburg.

33. To Ella Watson from camp near Fredericksburg, Virginia, December 21, 1862.

34. To William Hartley Watson from camp near Fredericksburg, Virginia, December 28, 1862. McClellan would probably have done well in a staff post like Halleck's. Major Watson's suggestion seems sensible.

1863

1. To Ella Watson from camp near Fredericksburg, Virginia, January 4, 1863.

2. To William Hartley Watson from camp near Fredericksburg, Virginia, January 15, 1863.

3. To Ella Watson from camp near Fredericksburg, Virginia, January 17, 1863.

4. To William Hartley Watson from camp near Fredericksburg, Virginia, January 19, 1863. At this point Major Watson had had no pay since joining the regiment four months before.

5. To Emma Watson from camp near Fredericksburg, Virginia, January 27, 1863.

6. Ibid., January 30, 1863.

7. To William Hartley Watson from camp near Fredericksburg, Virginia, February 2, 1863.

8. To William Hartley Watson from camp of the 105th Regiment, February 3, 1863.

9. To William Hartley Watson from Division Hospital, March 8, 1863.

10. To Eliza Watson from camp near Potomac Creek, Virginia, April 6, 1863.

11. To Emma Watson from camp near Potomac Creek, Virginia, April 18, 1863. Brigadier General Charles K. Graham commanded the 1st Brigade of the 1st Division, 3rd Corps, Army of the Potomac.

12. To Eliza Watson from camp near Potomac Creek, Virginia, April 23, 1863. At Kelly's Ford, Virginia, on April 17, eight Union regiments and one battery had collided with Stuart's cavalry in a series of skirmishes.

13. To William Hartley Watson from camp near the Rappahannock River, Virginia, April 30, 1863. Brigadier General Alfred Pleasonton was a cavalry commander in the Army of the Potomac. The rumor of his death was erroneous. He saw active service until the cavalry corps was broken up in May 1865. Major General John Sedgwick, commander of the 6th Corps, Army of the Potomac, was killed at Spotsylvania in May 1864.

14. To William Hartley Watson from battlefield, May 5, 1863.

15. To William Hartley Watson from camp near Potomac Creek, Virginia, May 7, 1863.

16. Ibid., May 8, 1863. At this time the 105th Regiment, along with the 57th, 63rd, 68th, 114th, and 141st Pennsylvania, was in the 1st Brigade, Brigadier General Charles K. Graham; 1st Division, Brigadier General David B. Birney; 3rd Corps, Major General Daniel E. Sickles. Gordon W. Jones notes that Watson's description of his field hospital as "on the plank road ten miles south of Chancellorsville" would locate it miles behind Lee's lines. This, Jones suggests, indicates that some of Watson's letters may have been written from memory some time after the fact, possibly to replace lost letters (*Virginia Magazine of History and Biography,* 1962, 214).

17. To Charlotte Watson from camp near Potomac Creek, Virginia, May 15, 1863.

18. To William Hartley Watson from camp near Potomac Creek, Virginia, May 17, 1863.

19. To Eliza Watson from camp near Potomac Creek, Virginia, May 26, 1863.

20. To William Hartley Watson from camp near Belle Plain, Virginia, June 4, 1863. The fear of "miasmatic fever" stemmed from a belief widely held at the time that disease was the result of noxious emanations from decaying vegetable matter in swamps. No doubt the fever was malarial, disseminated by those mosquitoes.

21. To Emma Watson from camp near Belle Plain, Virginia, June 5, 1863.

22. To William Hartley Watson from camp near Belle Plain, Virginia, June 9, 1863. Despite the major's belief that he "had nothing interesting to write," the reader of his letters more than one hundred years later may conclude that he generally made them lively.

23. To William Hartley Watson from camp near Gum Spring, Virginia, June 24, 1863. Gum Spring is near Louisa, about eight miles south of the North Anna River. Bloody Run, in southern Pennsylvania, is about forty-five miles north of Winchester, Virginia.

24. To William Hartley Watson from camp near Gettysburg, Pennsylvania, July 7, 1863. This letter is written in a hand different from Major Watson's, which suggests that he dictated it to a clerk, perhaps because he was too busy or too tired to push a pen.

25. Ibid., July 9, 1863. Dr. Jonathan Letterman, organizer of the field medical service of Union armies, had been promoted to the rank of major in 1862 and made medical director of the Army of the Potomac. Major General John A. Dix commanded the 7th Corps, Army of the Potomac; Major General William H. French assumed command of the 3rd Corps after Sickles became a casualty at Gettysburg.

26. To William Hartley Watson from 1st Division, 3rd Corps Hospital near Gettysburg, Pennsylvania, July 18, 1863.

27. To Emma Watson from Hospital 1st Division, 3rd Corps near Gettysburg, Pennsylvania, July 20, 1863.

28. To Charlotte Watson from camp near Culpeper, Virginia, September 27, 1863.

29. To William Hartley Watson from Fairfax Station, Virginia, October 18, 1863; and camp near Catlett's Station, Virginia, October 21, 1863.

30. To Marie Watson from camp near Brandy Station, Virginia. This letter was dated November 19, 1864, in the 1961 edition of this book, which is probably mistaken. Gordon W. Jones finds it unlikely that Watson would be "transferred in a week from the Petersburg trenches of November 1864 to winter quarters at Brandy Station north of the Rapidan" (*The Virginia Magazine of History and Biography* [April 1962], 214). Professor Robert E. May of Purdue University seconds this opinion, citing evidence in E. B. Long, *The Civil War Day by Day: An Almanac, 1861–1865* (Garden City, N. Y.: Doubleday, 1971); and Angus Johnston, *Virginia Railroads in the Civil War* (Chapel Hill: Published for the Virginia Historical Society by the University of North Carolina Press, 1961).

31. To Emma Watson from camp near Brandy Station, Virginia, November 24, 1863.

32. To William Hartley Watson from camp near Brandy Station, Virginia, December 4, 1863. Major General Gouverneur K. Warren, chief

engineer of the Army of the Potomac, commanded the 2nd Corps at Mine Run and other engagements in December 1863.

33. To Charlotte Watson from camp near Brandy Station, Virginia, December 13, 1863.

1864

1. To William Hartley Watson from Pittsburgh, Pennsylvania, February 11, 1864.

2. To William Hartley Watson from camp near Culpeper, Virginia, February 23, 1864.

3. Ibid., March 3, 1864.

4. To William Hartley Watson from camp near Brandy Station, Virginia, April 6, 1864.

5. To William Hartley Watson from hospital on battlefield, May 7, 1864. The killed and wounded mentioned by Major Watson were all officers of the 105th Regiment.

6. To "Doctor" from Hospital 3rd Division, 2nd Corps, May 19, 1864. This letter, in a hand different from Major Watson's, was probably written by a company clerk.

7. To William Hartley Watson from White House, Virginia, June 1, 1864.

8. To William Hartley Watson from Hospital 3rd Division, 2nd Corps, August 19, 1864.

9. To Marie Watson from Hospital 3rd Division, 2nd Corps, September 4, 1864. Captain Charles E. Patton commanded Company C of the 105th Regiment.

10. To William Hartley Watson from Hospital 3rd Division, 2nd Corps, City Point, Virginia, September 30, 1864.

11. Ibid., October 24, 1864.

12. To Emma Watson from Hospital 3rd Division, 2nd Corps, City Point, Virginia, October 29, 1864.

13. To William Hartley Watson from Hospital 3rd Division, 2nd Corps, City Point, Virginia, October 30, 1864. On October 27, at Hatcher's Run, two divisions of the 2nd Corps, together with the 5th

and 9th Corps and the cavalry of General Gregg, attempted to turn the enemy's right flank, but failed with casualties of about 2,000.

14. To Emma Watson from Hospital 3rd Division, 2nd Corps, City Point, Virginia, November 6, 1864.

15. To William Hartley Watson from Hospital 3rd Division, 2nd Corps, City Point, Virginia, November 12, 1864.

1865

1. To William Hartley Watson from camp of the 105th Pennsylvania Volunteers, January 29, 1865.

2. To William Hartley Watson from camp near Petersburg, Virginia, February 25, 1865. Major Watson had an unfortunate time with his horses.

3. To William Hartley Watson from Headquarters, 2nd Brigade, near Petersburg, Virginia, March 18, 1865.

4. To William Hartley Watson from Headquarters, 2nd Brigade, 3rd Division, 2nd Corps, Burkesville Station, Virginia, April 18, 1865.

5. Ibid., April 27, 1865.

6. To Charlotte Watson from Headquarters, 2nd Brigade, 3rd Division, 2nd Corps, Burkesville Junction, Virginia, April 28, 1865. Major Watson's reasoning on the legal ownership of the captured horse is ingenious. But whether or not he was permitted to take this mount home with him is not revealed.

7. To William Hartley Watson from Headquarters, 105th Pennsylvania Volunteers, May 2, 1865.

8. To Emma Watson from camp near Alexandria, Virginia, May 15, 1865.

9. To Marie Watson from camp near Washington, D.C., May 21, 1865.

Bibliography

Unpublished Material

Letters of Major William Watson, Surgeon, 105th Regiment of Pennsylvania Volunteers, Army of the Potomac, 1862–65.

Books and Articles

The American Heritage Picture History of the Civil War. New York, 1960.

Dowdey, Clifford. *Experiment in Rebellion.* New York, 1946.

————. *Lee's Last Campaign.* Boston, 1960.

Fatout, Paul. "The California Regiment, Colonel Baker, and Ball's Bluff." *California Historical Society Quarterly* 31, no. 3 (September 1952): 229–40.

The Medical and Surgical History of the War of the Rebellion. 6 vols. Prepared by Surgeon General Joseph K. Barnes, United States Army. Washington, D.C., 1870–83.

The Photographic History of the Civil War. 10 vols. Edited by Francis Trevelyan Miller. New York, 1911.

Randall, J. G. *Lincoln the President.* 2 vols. New York, 1945.

The Rebellion Record. 9 vols. New York, 1862–67.

Scott, Kate M. *History of the One Hundred and Fifth Regiment of Pennsylvania Volunteers.* Philadelphia, 1877.

The War of the Rebellion: A Compilation of the Official Records of the Union and Confederate Armies. Washington, D. C., 1880–1901.

Index

Abolitionists, 88–89
Accidents, as self-mutilations, 88
African Americans: contrabands, 14, 80; as Union troops, 79–81, 83
Aldie, Va., 106, 107
Ambulances: lack at Chancellorsville, 91–92; as transportation, 16, 35–36
Amputation instruments, as booty, 146
Amputations, 91–92, 97, 108, 110
Antietam, Battle of, 19, 28, 45
Appomattox, 144
Armistice, rumors of, 49, 51
Army of Northern Virginia (CSA), 30; in the Wilderness, 126, 139; invasion of Pennsylvania, 105; surrender of, 144

Army of the Potomac (USA): at Chancellorsville, 89–99; at Gettysburg, 107, 108–11; in late 1862, 14; and political military appointments, 26–27; politicking in, 13. *See also* Fredericksburg; 105th Regiment; Wilderness campaign
Army of the Trans-Mississippi (CSA), 152
Assistant surgeon, first. *See* Ewing, George
Assistant surgeons, 13, 16

Badges, Army, for corps and divisions, 97, 132
Baker, E. D. (gen., USA), 32
Ball's Bluff, Battle of, 32–33
Baltimore, Md., 105
Bands, army, 21